THE GRAPES OF WRATH

AUTHORED by Jeremy Ross
UPDATED AND REVISED by Caroline Lauer

COVER DESIGN by Table XI Partners LLC
COVER PHOTO by Olivia Verma and © 2005 GradeSaver, LLC

BOOK DESIGN by Table XI Partners LLC

Published by GradeSaver LLC, www.gradesaver.com

First published in the United States of America by GradeSaver LLC. 2014

ISBN 978-1-60259-543-9

Printed in the United States of America

Table of Contents

Biography of John Steinbeck (1902–1968)

John Steinbeck was born in Salinas, California in 1902. He spent most of his life in Monterey County, which is the setting for much of his fiction. He attended Stanford University intermittently between 1920 and 1926. Steinbeck did not graduate from Stanford, but instead chose to support himself by doing manual labor while writing in his spare time. His experiences among the working class of California lends authenticity to his depiction of the lives of laborers, who are the central characters in many of his most celebrated novels.

Steinbeck's first novel, *Cup of Gold*, was published in 1929. It was followed by *The Pastures of Heaven* and, in 1933, *To a God Unknown*. However, his first three novels were unsuccessful both critically and commercially. Steinbeck had his first success with *Tortilla Flat* (1935), an affectionate and gently humorous story about Mexican-Americans. Meanwhile, his subsequent novel, *In Dubious Battle* (1936) is renowned for its markedly grim outlook. This novel is a classic account of a strike by agricultural laborers and the pair of Marxist labor organizers who engineer it, and is the first Steinbeck novel to display the striking social commentary that characterizes his most notable works. Steinbeck received even greater acclaim for the novella *Of Mice and Men* (1937), a tragic story about a strange and complex bond between two migrant laborers. His crowning achievement, *The Grapes of Wrath* (1939), won Steinbeck a Pulitzer Prize and a National Book Award. It was also adapted into a classic film directed by John Ford, which the American Film Institute has since called one of the greatest films of all time. *Grapes of Wrath* chronicles the migration of a dispossessed family from the Oklahoma Dust Bowl to California and critiques their subsequent exploitation by a ruthless system of agricultural economics.

After the best-selling success of *The Grapes of Wrath*, Steinbeck went to Mexico to collect marine life with the freelance biologist Edward F. Ricketts. The two men collaborated on *Sea of Cortez* (1941), a study of the fauna of the Gulf of California. During World War II, Steinbeck wrote some effective pieces of government propaganda, among them *The Moon Is Down* (1942), a novel about Norwegians under the Nazis. He also served as a war correspondent. With the end of World War II and the move from the Great Depression to economic prosperity in America, Steinbeck's work softened somewhat. While they still contain the elements of social criticism that mark his earlier work, the three novels Steinbeck published immediately following the war, *Cannery Row* (1945), *The Pearl*, and *The Bus* (both 1947) are more sentimental and relaxed. Steinbeck also contributed to several screenplays. He wrote the original stories for a number of films, including *Lifeboat* (1944), directed by Alfred Hitchcock, and *A Medal for Benny.* He also wrote the screenplay for Elia Kazan's *Viva Zapata!*, a biographical film about Emiliano Zapata, the Mexican peasant who was the leader of the revolution in the state of Morelos.

Steinbeck married Carol Henning in 1930 and they lived together in Pacific Grove, California. During this time, Steinbeck spent a great deal of time in Monterey with Ed Ricketts at his Cannery Row laboratory. This experience inspired his popular 1945 novel, *Cannery Row*. In 1943, Steinbeck married his second wife, Gwyndolyn Conger, with whom he had two children. 1948 was a particularly bad year for Steinbeck: Ricketts died, and Gwyndolyn left him. However, he found happiness once again in 1950 when he married Elaine Scott and moved to New York City. Two years later, he published the highly controversial *East of Eden*, the novel Steinbeck referred to as "the big one." It is set in California's Salinas Valley.

Steinbeck's later works were comparatively slight, but he did make several notable attempts to reassert his stature as a major novelist, writing *Burning Bright* (1950), *East of Eden* (1952), and *The Winter of Our Discontent* (1961). However, none of these works garnered the critical esteem of his earlier novels. Steinbeck's enduring legacy is still the naturalistic, proletarian-themed novels that he wrote during the Depression. Steinbeck received the Nobel Prize for literature in 1962. He died in New York City in 1968.

In 2012, as is the custom, the Swedish Academy (who awards the Nobel Prize) released the official documentation of their deliberations for the 1962 Nobel Prize. The documents reveal that Steinbeck was not a clear choice, but rather, the Academy members were trying to "make the best of a bad situation." A New York Times article claims, "the decision came amid their general dissatisfaction with the candidates for the prize that year, according to documents recently released by the academy." Besides Steinbeck, the other writers that the Swedish Academy considered in 1962 were Robert Graves, Lawrence Durrell, Karen Blixen, and Jean Anouilh. While the documents reveal that the committee was not excited about Steinbeck as a choice, they did not give this impression in their public statements about Steinbeck. After Steinbeck's win was announced, the Academy released a statement saying that he was among "the masters of modern American literature" because of "his realistic as well as imaginative writings, distinguished by a sympathetic humor and a keen social perception."

The Grapes of Wrath Study Guide

Published in 1939, John Steinbeck's *The Grapes of Wrath* was met with immediate critical and popular success when it first appeared. An American realist novel set during the Great Depression and the Dust Bowl, Steinbeck's work documents hard times in general, and also explores its era through the experiences of one particular family, the Joads. Steinbeck focuses throughout on the oppression of poor tenant farmers by industrialized agriculture: he depicts the hardships that such farmers experience at the hands of callous, wealthy, and greedy landowners. Yet *The Grapes of Wrath* is also a story of man versus the environment, since the families depicted in its narrative have been forced to flee the poor agricultural conditions afflicting the Great Plains. Seeking better farming conditions and new land after being forced out by corporate agriculture, the former farmers have gathered their families and belongings in barely functional cars and have set out for California. Unfortunately, a better life does not await them, and they merely continue to struggle against corporate interests.

Steinbeck's novel confronted and exposed the difficulties faced by this landless population, and it argued persuasively for the need to organize labor forces. When he was preparing to publish the book, Steinbeck said, "I want to put a tag of shame on the greedy bastards who are responsible for this [the Great Depression and its effects]." After publication, he told a reporter that, "I've done my damndest to rip a reader's nerves to rags." Because of his staunch support for the working class, Steinbeck won the praise and admiration of this segment of society. Critically acclaimed, the novel itself won the National Book Award and the Pulitzer Prize for fiction the year immediately after its publication, 1940. The popular success of *The Grapes of Wrath* matched the critical praise, and Hollywood produced a 1940 film adaptation, which would become widely watched.

The Grapes of Wrath continues to influence readers and inspire student discussions, even though the history it addresses is far in the past. It is still one of the most widely read novels in both high school and college classrooms. The novel has even continued to prompt further research: just recently, the Steinbeck Institute commissioned researchers to trace the path of the Joads. They reported that little has changed -- a traveler who sets out from Oklahoma and heads for California is met with wide expanses and difficult terrain, much the same landscape that the Joads encountered. In more ways than one, *The Grapes of Wrath* is timeless.

The Grapes of Wrath Summary

John Steinbeck's novel *The Grapes of Wrath* tells the specific story of the Joad family, and thus illustrates the hardships and oppression suffered by migrant laborers during the Great Depression. It is an explicitly political piece of writing, one that champions collective action by the lower classes. In taking this social stance, Steinbeck's novel criticizes shortsighted self-interest and chastises corporate and banking elites for profit-maximizing policies that ultimately forced farmers into destitution and even starvation.

The novel begins with a description of the conditions in Dust Bowl Oklahoma that ruined crops and instigated massive foreclosures on farmland. No specific characters emerge initially; this is a technique that Steinbeck will employ several times in the book, posing descriptions of events in a large social context against descriptions of events more particular to the Joad family.

Tom Joad, a man not yet thirty, approaches a diner dressed in spotless, somewhat formal clothing. He hitches a ride with a truck driver, who presses Tom for information until Tom finally reveals that he was just released from McAlester prison, where he served four years for murdering a man during a fight. Steinbeck follows this exchange with an interlude describing a turtle crossing the road, which serves as a metaphor for the struggles of the working class.

On his travels home, Tom meets a onetime preacher, Jim Casy, a talkative man gripped by doubts over religious teachings and the presence of sin. He gave up the ministry after realizing that he found little wrong with the sexual liaisons he had with the women in his congregation. Casy espouses the view that what is holy in human nature comes not from a distant God, but from people themselves. Steinbeck contrasts Tom's return with the arrival of bank representatives to evict the tenant farmers. The possibility of a working class insurrection is raised, but an effective target for collective action cannot be found.

Tom and Casy reach the Joads' house, only to find that it has been deserted. Muley Graves, a local elderly man who may not be sane, tells them that the Joads have been evicted, and that the family now stays with Uncle John. Muley's own family has left to find work in California, but Muley decided to stay himself.

Steinbeck then provides a description of the tactics that car dealers use to exploit impoverished customers. The dealers find that they can make greater profits by selling damaged jalopies than by selling dependable new cars.

Tom Joad finds the rest of his family staying with Uncle John, a morose man who has been prone to depression since the death of his wife several years earlier. Yet Tom's mother is a strong, sturdy woman who is the moral center of family life. His brother, Noah, may have been brain damaged during childbirth, while his sister, Rose of Sharon (called Rosasharn by the family) is recently married and pregnant. Her husband, Connie Rivers, has dreams of studying radios. Tom's younger brother, Al, is only sixteen. This introduction to Steinbeck's characters is followed by a more general description of the sale of items by impoverished families who intend to leave Oklahoma for California, as the Joads expect to do.

The Joads plan to go to California on account of flyers advertising work in the California fields. These flyers, as Steinbeck will soon reveal, are fraudulent advertisements meant to draw more workers than necessary and drive down wages. Jim Casy asks to accompany the Joads to California so that he can work with the people in the fields rather than preach at them. Before the family leaves, Grampa Joad declares his refusal to go, but the family gives him medicine to knock him unconscious and takes him along. The subsequent chapters describe the vacant houses that remain after the Oklahoma farmers have left for work elsewhere, as well as the conditions on Route 66, the highway that stretches from Oklahoma to Bakersfield, California.

Almost immediately after the journey begins, the Joad family loses two members. The first victim is the family dog, which is run over during the Joads' first stop. The second is Grampa Joad, who dies of a stroke. The Wilson family helps the Joads when Grampa dies, and the two families decide to make the journey to California together. Steinbeck follows this with a larger statement about the growing of a collective consciousness among the working class, who shift their perceptions from "I" to "we."

The Wilsons' car soon breaks down, and Tom and Casy consider separating from the rest of the family temporarily to fix the car, but Ma Joad refuses to let the family break apart even for a short time. Tom and Al do find the necessary part to fix the car at a junkyard. Before the Joads set out on their journey again, they find a man returning from California, who tells them that there is no work there and that the promises of work in the flyers are all fraudulent.

The Joads and Wilsons reach California, where they are immediately subjected to intimidation by police officers who derisively call them, and other migrant laborers, "Okies." At the first camp where the Joads stay, Granma becomes quite ill, but receives some comfort from proselytizing Jehovites who merely annoy Ma Joad. The next time the police stop the Joads on their travels, Ma Joad forces the authorities to let the family pass without inspection. She does this to conceal the fact that Granma has died.

Steinbeck follows this with a description of the history of California, which has apparently been marked by oppression and slavery. However, he predicts an imminent revolution, for the people there have been deprived to such a great degree that they must at some point take whatever they need in order to survive.

At the next camp where the Joads stay in their search for work, they learn about Weedpatch, a government camp where the residents are spared harassment by police officers and have access to amenities such as baths and toilets. Later, when police officers attempt to start a fight with Tom and several other migrant workers, Tom trips an officer and Casy knocks him unconscious. To keep Tom from taking the blame (and from consequently being sent back to jail for violating his parole), Casy accepts responsibility for the crime and is taken away to jail. The rest of the family begins to break apart as well. Uncle John leaves to get drunk, Noah decides to leave society altogether and live alone in the woodlands, and Connie abandons his pregnant wife. Before they must move on, Tom does retrieve Uncle John, who is still consumed with guilt over his wife's death. They head north toward the government camp.

At the government camp, the Joads are shocked to find how well the other residents treat them and how efficiently this society (which even features democratic elections) functions. Tom also finds work quickly, but the contractor, Mr. Thomas, warns him that there will be trouble at the dance at Weedpatch that weekend. Since the police can only enter the camp if there is trouble, they intend to plant intruders there who will instigate violence.

The Joads settle into a comfortable existence at the government camp, and during the dance that Saturday, Tom and several other residents defuse the situation, preventing the police from taking control of the camp. Nevertheless, after a month in Weedpatch none of the Joads have found steady work; the family members realize that they must continue on their journey. They arrive at Hooper Ranch, where the entire family picks peaches. The wages they receive are higher than normal, for they are breaking a strike. Tom finds out that the leader of the labor force that is organizing the strike is Jim Casy. After spending time in prison, Casy realized that he must fight for collective action by the working class against the wealthy ruling class; Tom decides to join Casy in his efforts. Yet Tom, Casy, and the other strike leaders get into a fight with strike breakers, one of whom murders Casy with a pick. Tom struggles with the man and wrests away the weapon. He, in turn, kills the man who murdered Casy, and barely escapes capture by the police.

Although Tom wishes to leave the family in order to save them from taking responsibility for his actions, the Joads nevertheless decide to leave Hooper Ranch for a location where Tom can be safe. They reach cotton fields up north, where Tom hides in the woods while the family stays in a boxcar. Although the family attempts to keep Tom's identity and location a secret, young Ruthie Winfield reveals it during a fight with another child. When Ma tells Tom about this, he decides to leave the family and go off alone, determined to fight for the cause for which Casy died. He vows to return to his family one day.

The rainy season arrives almost immediately after Tom leaves the family; massive flooding results from this weather. The Joads are caught in a dangerous situation: they cannot escape the flooding because Rose of Sharon suddenly goes into labor. While other families evacuate the camp near the rapidly rising creek, the Joads remain and attempt to stop the flood waters. Without the aid of others, the Joads are unsuccessful, and they must seek refuge on the top of their car. Rose of Sharon delivers a stillborn child that Uncle John sends in a box down the creek. The family eventually reaches higher ground and finds a barn for shelter. Inside the barn is a starving man and his young son. Steinbeck ends the novel with Rose of Sharon, barely recovered from the delivery, breastfeeding the dying man to nurse him back to health.

The Grapes of Wrath Characters

Tom Joad

The central character of the novel, Tom is a recently-released inmate who returns home to find that his family has lost their farm and is moving west to California. He is a plainspoken and forthright man, yet he still retains some of his violent tendencies.

Ma Joad

The mother of Noah, Tom, Rose of Sharon, Ruthie, and Winfield, Ma Joad is a woman accustomed to hardship and deprivation. She is a forceful individual who is determined to keep her family together at nearly any cost; however, she shows kindness to outsiders, even sparing what little the Joad family has for those even less fortunate.

Pa Joad

Although Pa Joad is the head of the Joad household, he is not a particularly commanding presence. Without the ability to provide for his family, he recedes into the background, taking little initiative in deciding the fate of his relatives.

Uncle John

A morose man prone to depression and alcoholism, Uncle John believes that he is the cause of the family's misfortunes. He blames himself for the death of his wife, which took place several years before the story begins, and carries the guilt of that event with him.

Rose of Sharon

Tom Joad's younger sister, recently married to Connie Rivers and pregnant with Connie's child, Rose of Sharon is the one adult who retains a sense of optimism. She dreams of a middle-class life with her husband and child, but becomes paranoid and disillusioned when her husband abandons her upon reaching California.

Connie Rivers

The shiftless husband of Rose of Sharon, Connie dreams of taking correspondence courses that will provide him with job opportunities and the possibility of a better life. When he reaches California and does not find work, he immediately becomes disillusioned and abandons his pregnant wife.

Noah Joad

Tom's older brother, Noah suffers from mental disabilities that can probably be traced to his birth. He leaves the family to live in isolation from society, supporting himself by catching fish.

Al Joad

Al is Tom's younger brother; at sixteen years old, he is concerned with cars and girls, and remains combative toward the rest of the family. Of the Joad family members, Al has the most knowledge of cars, and fears that the rest of the family will blame him if anything goes wrong. He dreams of becoming a mechanic and becomes engaged to Aggie Wainwright by the end of the novel.

Ruthie Joad

One of the two small children in the Joad family, it is Ruthie who reveals that Tom is responsible for the murder at Hooper Ranch; this disclosure forces Tom to leave his family in order to escape capture by the police.

Winfield Joad

The other small child in the Joad family, Winfield becomes severely ill from deprivation, but survives his illness.

Grampa Joad

An energetic, feisty old man, Grampa refuses to leave Oklahoma with the rest of his family, but is forcibly taken on the journey after he is drugged by the other family members. Soon afterward, unable to bear leaving the area where he had long lived, Grampa dies of a stroke.

Granma Joad

Granma Joad does not survive much longer than her husband. She becomes severely ill on the journey to California, and dies not long after her family reaches the state.

Reverend Jim Casy

A onetime preacher who too often succumbed to temptation, Casy left the ministry when he realized that he did not believe in absolute ideas of sin. He espouses the idea that all that is holy comes from collective society, a belief that he puts into practice when, after spending time in jail, he becomes involved with labor activists. Casy is a martyr for his beliefs, murdered during a confrontation with police.

Muley Graves

Muley is a crazy elderly man who reveals to Tom Joad the fate of the Joad family. Having lost their home and farmland, Muley's wife and children left Oklahoma for California, but Muley decided to remain; he attempts to elude the police (who could arrest him for trespassing) and to live outside of society.

Sairy Wilson

Sairy and her family aid the Joads when Grampa Joad has a stroke; the Wilsons then decide to continue with the Joads on the way to California, since the two families can help each other during the journey. Sairy falls ill at the first camp where the two families stay and remains there with the rest of her family, facing the possibility of arrest for trespassing.

The Mayor

The Mayor is a half-crazed old migrant worker who has had to endure continued torture by the California police.

Floyd Knowles

Floyd befriends Al Joad and tells the Joad family about work opportunities, and about the government camp at Weedpatch.

Timothy and Wilkie Wallace

These two brothers are Weedpatch camp residents who take Tom to find work.

Mr. Thomas

The contractor who hires Tom and the Wallaces, Mr. Thomas warns the men about the intruders who will interrupt the dance at the government camp.

Jessie Bullitt

Jessie is the head of the Ladies Committee at Weedpatch; she gives Ma Joad a tour of the facilities.

Ella Summers

Ella is the assistant to Jessie Bullitt and a former head of the Ladies Committee; she frequently bickers with Jessie over insignificant details.

Jim Rawley

Jim is the manager of the camp at Weedpatch, and he treats the Joads with unexpected respect.

Lisbeth Sandry

Lisbeth is a fundamentalist zealot who complains about the alleged sins that take place at the government camp, including dancing. She frightens Rose of Sharon with her admonitions about sin.

Ezra Huston

Ezra is the elected head of the Central Committee at Weedpatch. He advises Tom and the other men on how to deal with the situation at the Saturday dance.

Willie Eaton

Willie is the head of the Weedpatch entertainment committee. He defuses the problem raised by the intruders and the police during the dance.

Aggie Wainwright

Aggie is the young woman to whom Al Joad becomes engaged.

The Grapes of Wrath Glossary

blazon

(v.) - with object

1. [with adverbial of place] to display prominently or vividly

Ex: They saw their company name blazoned all over the media.

2. to describe or depict (armorial bearings) in a correct heraldic manner

embalm

(v.)

to preserve from decay, originally with spices but now usually through the arterial injection of a preservative

Ex: They tried to embalm the body, but they did not have the resources they needed.

gasket

(n.)

1. a shaped piece or ring of rubber or other material sealing the junction between two surfaces in an engine or other device

2. a cord securing a furled sail to the yard, boom, or gaff of a sailing vessel

Ex: The gasket in his car was in need of repair.

gopher

(n.)

a burrowing rodent with fur-lined pouches on the outsides of the cheeks, found in North and Central America

Ex: Their backyard was infested with gophers.

handbill

(n.)

a small printed advertisement or other notice distributed by hand

Ex: They stood on the street and distributed handbills to everyone who passed them by.

haycock

(n.)

a conical heap of hay in a field

Ex: After an afternoon of work, the farmers had gathered enough hay to create a haycock.

inquisitive

(adj.)

curious or inquiring

Ex: He was very inquisitive, always asking new questions about his surroundings.

jalopy

(n.)

an old car in a dilapidated condition

Ex: Rusted jalopies filled the junkyard.

noose

(n.)

a loop with a running knot, tightening as the rope or wire is pulled and typically used to hang people or trap animals

Ex: The farmer used a noose to catch the raccoon that had been eating his plants.

parole

(n.)

the release of a prisoner temporarily (for a special purpose) or permanently before the completion of a sentence, on the promise of good behavior

Ex: Although the authorities released him on parole, he committed a burglary and was sent back to prison.

picket

(n.)

1. a person or group of people standing outside a place of work or other venue, protesting about something or trying to persuade others not to enter during a strike

2. a soldier or party of soldiers performing a particular duty

3. a pointed wooden stake driven into the ground, typically to form a fence or palisade, or to tether a horse

profit margin

(n.)

the amount by which revenue from sales exceeds costs in a business

Ex: The store owner only cared about his profit margin; he had little regard for how he treated his employees.

prophecy

(n.)

a prediction

Ex: He delivered a bleak prophecy of war and ruin.

scowl

(n.)

an angry or bad-tempered expression

Ex: A scowl overtook his face when he saw his enemy.

(v.)

to frown in an angry or bad-tempered way

Ex: My younger brother scowled at me after I took his toy.

scrounge

(v.)

to seek to obtain at the expense of or through the generosity of others, or simply by stealth

Ex: He managed to scrounge a free meal.

slop

(v.)

1. to spill or flow over the edge of a container, typically as the result of careless handling

2. [with object] to feed slops to an animal, especially a pig

3. [no obj.] to speak or write in a sentimentally effusive manner; to gush

tar and feather

(phrase)

to smear with tar and then cover with feathers as a punishment

Ex: In one of their favorite forms of public humiliation, the British tarred and feathered their enemies.

tarpaulin

(n.)

a heavy-duty waterproof cloth, originally made of tarred canvas

Ex: They covered the shelves with a tarpaulin.

upholstery

(n.)

a soft, padded textile covering that is fixed to furniture such as armchairs and sofas

Ex: The old couch had torn upholstery.

wizened

(adj.)

shriveled or wrinkled with age

Ex: He was a wizened, weather-beaten old man.

The Grapes of Wrath Themes

Commonality of Experience

The beauty of *The Grapes of Wrath* is that the experiences of the Joads speak for the experiences of thousands of other families traveling west in search of a better life. Such commonality of experience exists in the historical content that is laid out at the beginning of the novel, and also occurs within the novel's architecture itself. Steinbeck's novel transitions between chapters that detail the lives of the Joads and the chapters that deal with migrants more generally. It is in these chapters, which discuss broader currents and trends, that the commonality of experience truly shines through. These portions of the narrative are especially effective in communicating this theme because they always preface the more detailed, Joad-oriented chapters; in essence, they set the stage for the particular aspects of the Joads' lives. In this way, the commonality of experience adds gravity and importance to Steinbeck's *The Grapes of Wrath*, assuring it a place among great and resonant works of American literature.

Corporate Greed

Progressing hand-in-hand with the theme of industrialization, the idea of corporate greed is essential to the novel. This theme even ties in directly with the title: the phrase "grapes of wrath" can be found in both the Book of Revelation and the Battle Hymn of the Republic. Both of these references, as understood in Steinbeck's context, amount to a call for a higher power to right the wrongs that the corporate powers have done to the landless farmers. The greed of wealthy landowners is showcased from the beginning of the novel to the end -- they are ruthless and will do anything for higher profit margins.

This mentality is evident both in the general narrative chapters and in the chapters that deal specifically with the Joads and their direct acquaintances. At the hands of greedy landowners, people like the Joads lead pitiful and difficult lives. They are barely able to feed themselves on their daily wages, and the living conditions they face are horrible. Hundreds of thousands of people suffer just so a few corporate powers can make more money off another box of peaches or another pound of cotton. Under the pressure of these working conditions, the "grapes of wrath" of the laborers ferment and grow bitterly strong.

Industrialization

The heavy industrialization of American farming has enabled high-profile, wealthy landowners to extract greater profits from the land. These powerful landowners do not need to treat laborers well if they can opt to have efficient tractors plow the acres under their control. Along with industrialization, the creation of high-powered machines has enabled corporate interests to move laborers off the land and render them irrelevant.

Furthermore, industrialization has led to a farming and economic process that involves both vertical integration and horizontal integration. (Vertical integration occurs when the supply chain of a company is also owned by that company -- for example, the peach cannery also owns the farm where the peaches come from. Horizontal integration occurs when a company expands across an entire industry, acquiring several individual entities in a field of work. For example, this occurs when an especially powerful farmer is able to push fellow farmers out of business.) When both of these processes occur simultaneously, monopolies are able to grow and become very powerful.

Man's Connection to the Land

The farmer's, and man's, connection to the land is an important theme in *The Grapes of Wrath*. When the people of Oklahoma are forced to leave their land, this process proves to be devastating. These farmers have been a part of their land and have felt deeply connected to it for years: their hopes and dreams were lost or won in the soil, but now an inanimate tractor plows their onetime territory. The man who drives the tractor never touches the soil or interacts with it, which is a travesty according to the farmers. When the farmers leave, they lose part of themselves. But even beyond the difficulty of leaving their original land, the farmers are unable to create new connections with new land. They are forced to stay on the road, with no places to sleep or live, constantly moving. They are unable to put down roots, and such dislocation is particularly difficult considering their prior connections to set, customary ways of life.

Organized Labor

As the farmers become aware of the injustices that they continue to endure at the hands of the corporate powers, they also realize the futility of the actions of lone individuals. An individual farmer cannot even support his family and buy them food for dinner after a long day of work, and such a farmer's wages could continue to decrease at the whim of the landowners. (There is no incentive for the owners to provide a living wage when there is no organized resistance to their manner of operating.) If the workers can come together and communicate with one another, there is a possibility that they can stand up to the forces of corporate greed. If they do not stand together, they will continue to undercut one another and their wages will continue to fall. By organizing formally and by refusing to accept unfairly low wages, the laborers are able to exhibit their own form of power.

In the novel, organized workers are frequently called "reds" or Communists, but genuine labor organization (which often uses democratic structures and procedures) is a far cry from Communism.

Hope versus Hopelessness

As the Joads travel across the country, they remain unsure of what they will experience when they arrive in California. Each of the Joads deals with such uncertainty in a different way; however, regardless of whether they discuss the future or remain silent about it, there is an element of hope within all of the members of the family. They believe that they are starting out on a journey towards a new and better life. The men have hope that they will find work, Ma has hope that she will have a white house, and Rose of Sharon has hope that she will live in a town with an ice box and easy access to a movie theater.

The Joads maintain this sense of hope despite the fact that they inhabit a world that offers few reasons for optimism. Even as they face immense difficulties in their everyday lives -- work is not easy to find, food is expensive, and they are frequently forced to move from one place to another -- they maintain this positive outlook. When the men pull into the peach farm and begin to realize how difficult the work will be, Ma still believes that soon the Joads will save enough money to buy a house with some land. Their attitudes contrast with their environment, thus creating a tension between hope and hopelessness that emerges at different points throughout the novel.

Death and Suffering

Related to the theme of hope and hopelessness, the theme of death and suffering is essential to the difficult environment that the Joads face. Death is prevalent from the very beginning of the novel until the very end. Grampa dies on the first night of the trip, and Granma dies just as the Joads enter California. Even for the Joads who are relatively healthy, unpleasant conditions still abound. They cannot escape the elements and are barely able to eat. Rose of Sharon, who is pregnant, is unable to get the nutrients she needs for her baby, and her suffering is exacerbated by the journey as well.

Ultimately, the suffering of the Joads reflects the suffering of thousands of families traveling to California and looking for work. The bleak environment has been created by a variety of factors, the most prominent which are corporate greed and the industrialization of agriculture. Yet despite the prevalence of death and suffering, the Joads and many of the other traveling families try to maintain hope; they keep alive their belief in the American Dream and reassure themselves that a better life awaits them.

The Grapes of Wrath Quotes and Analysis

"'It's mine. I built it. You bump it down -- I'll be in the window with a rifle. You even come too close and I'll pot you like a rabbit.'

'It's not me. There's nothing I can do. I'll lose my job if I don't do it. And look -- suppose you kill me? They'll just hang you, but long before you're hung there'll be another guy on the tractor, and he'll bump the house down. You're not killing the right guy.'

'That's so,' the tenant said. 'Who gave you orders? I'll go after him. He's the one to kill.'

'You're wrong. He got his orders from the bank. The bank told him, "Clear those people out or it's your job."'

'Well, there's a president of the bank. There's a board of directors. I'll fill up the magazine of the rifle and go into the bank.'

The driver said, 'Fellow was telling me the bank gets orders from the East. The orders were, 'Make the land show profit or we'll close you up.'

'But where does it stop? Who can we shoot? I don't aim to starve to death before I kill the man that's starving me.'

'I don't know. Maybe there's nobody to shoot. Maybe the thing isn't men at all.'"

Tenant and Driver, p. 49

This dialogue involves two individuals who have not been formally introduced to us; like the other chapters devoted to unnamed characters, this chapter is posed against the narrative of Reverend Casy and Tom Joad. The namelessness of the two individuals creates a universalizing effect, since it is easy for the reader to believe that conversations like this are happening on farmlands across the United States. The tenant has a visceral reaction to the driver's threat to his home and livelihood, yet through this conversation the reader can see how the tenant's anger is misplaced and futile.

The destruction of the tenant's home is part of a much bigger, more comprehensive system than he can initially imagine. Shooting the driver will only lead to another driver taking his place, and the driver is merely responding to instructions from his supervisors, who are likewise responding to instructions from their supervisors. As this progression continues to unfold, the tenant becomes further and further removed from tangible possibilities for creating change. Through this conversation, Steinbeck portrays the situation of the tenant as hopeless; he illustrates how little power the tenant really has.

> *"An' then I'd want to go in town an' kill folks. 'Cause what'd they take when they tractored the folks off the lan'? What'd they get so their 'margin a profit' was safe? They got Pa dyin' on the groun', an' Joe yellin his first breath, an' me jerkin' like a billy goat under a bush in the night. What'd they get? God knows the land' ain't no good. Nobody been able to make a crop for years. But thems sons-a-bitches at their desks, they jus' chopped folks in tow for their margin a profit. They jus' cut 'em in two. Place were folks live is them folks. They ain't whole, out lonely on the road in a piled-up car. They ain't alive no more. Them sons-a-bitches killed 'em."*
>
> *Muley Graves, p. 67*

When Tom Joad realizes that his home has been abandoned, he and Casy become aware of how little they know about what has transpired on the land; they decide to stay with Muley Graves and hear what he has to say about everything. Muley is frustrated and lonely. While his relatives, who can no longer support themselves on the land, have left for California, Muley has stayed in order to watch over things. Slowly, he has realized the futility of trying to protect the land that was once his.

In this quote, Muley explains both his own, and the broader farmer population's, connection to the land. He sums up, in a simple yet profound way, the injustices of industrial agriculture and the corporate world's lack of compassion. Everything can be reduced to a bottom line, margin of profit, and there is no space for humanity in that equation. A callous and deeply unfair economic and agricultural system has pushed the people off the land and has taken away their means of survival.

> *"How can we live without our lives? How will we know it's us without our past? No. Leave it. Burn it. They sat and looked at it and burned it into their memories. How'll it be not to know what land's outside the door? How if you wake up in the night and know -- and know the willow tree's not there? Can you live without the willow tree? Well, no, you can't. The willow tree is you."*
>
> *Narrator, p. 114 - 115*

This quote is located in a chapter that deals with the broader struggle that the Joads are going through and that highlights the difficulties of saying goodbye to prized possessions and moving on to a new place. The challenges that the Joads and others in their situation face are not only economic but also emotional. It is clear that the family is leaving behind everything of both economic and sentimental value, in the hope that a better life awaits in California. Yet even if California is everything that the Joads have imagined, the trip and transition still require a remarkable amount of sacrifice. And even if the family members are able to create new lives for themselves, they have still left a part of themselves behind in the Oklahoma land that they once considered their property.

> *"One man, one family driven from the land; this rusty car creaking along the highway to the west. I lost my land, a single tractor took my land. I am alone and I am bewildered. And in the night one family camps in a ditch and another family pulls in and the tents come out. The two men squat on their hams and the women and children listen. Here is the node, you who hate change and fear revolution. Keep those two squatting men apart; make them hate, fear, suspect each other. Here is the anlage of the thing you fear. This is the zygote. For here "I lost my land" is changed; a cell is split and from its splitting grows the thing you hate -- "We lost our land." The danger is here, for two men are not as lonely and perplexed as one.*
>
> *Narrator, p. 194*

In this broad, generic chapter (which does not consider the Joads alone), the narrator speaks of the potential for underprivileged people to unite. When just one man realizes the unfairness of his personal life -- whether it's losing his land to a company with a tractor or having to overpay for a broken-down jalopy -- that man does not realize the systemic unfairness that affects everyone. The owner men and the other perpetrators of this systematic injustice want the individuals on the bottom to stay isolated and not interact with others. When these individuals go about their lives as separate persons, they lack the power and momentum to create change. Yet when they meet others with the same goals, the volume of their complaints grows -- as does their awareness of the extent of the injustices they face. The transition from "I" to "we" terrifies those who perpetuate economic inequality; with this shift, their system begins to become endangered.

> *"An' I wouldn't pray for a ol' fella that's dead. He's awright. He got a job to do, but it's all laid out for 'im an' there's on'y one way to do it. But us, we got a job to do, an' they's a thousan' ways, an' we don' know which one to take. An' if I was to pray, it'd be for the folks that don' know which way to turn. Grampa here, he got the easy straight. An' now cover 'im up and let 'im get to his work."*
>
> *Casy, p. 184 - 185*

When Casy delivers this "sermon" to the rest of the Joad group, he speaks to many of their fears of the future. They don't know what awaits them: even though they have been promised a fruitful future in California, doubts have started to creep in and new possibilities and alternatives have begun to multiply. Mirroring the many possibilities are the differing reactions of the members of the Joad family. Ma is calm and refuses to think much about the future, Pa remains preoccupied with the great things that await, and Tom refuses to engage in conversations about the future out of self-protection, since he doesn't want to be disappointed.

Overall, Casy believes that the people who have no clear direction in life are the ones who are in need of the prayers, so that such prayers are applicable to the Joads as they face an uncertain future. His message is important because it applies to all of the people moving to California -- not just to the Joads. Each traveler has a highly individualized image of the future, but nobody knows which image will become reality.

> *"S'pose you got a job a work, an' there's jus' one fella wants the job. You got to pay 'im what he asts. But s'pose they's a hunderd men." He put down his tool. His eyes hardened and his voice sharpened. "S'pose they's a hunderd men wants that job. S'pose them men got kids, an' them kids is hungry. S'pose a lousy dime'll buy a box a mush for them kids. S'pose a nickel'll buy at leas' somepin for them kids. An' you got a hunderd men. Jus' offer 'em a nickel - why, they'll kill each other fightin' for that nickel."*
>
> *Floyd, p. 315*

Whenever the Joads experience doubts about their prospects in California, they ease their worries to some extent by reminding themselves of the orange handbill that Pa carries in his coat. According to the handbill, hundreds of men are required for work in the fields; supposedly, the Joads can count on getting work and earning good wages as soon as they arrive in California. Yet when they arrive, they are not met with the bountiful opportunities that they had imagined, and a conversation with a man named Floyd (a leader of a migrant group) reveals why this is the case. With a surplus of laborers, who were unorganized and prone to infighting, the owners had the definitive advantage. They could dictate wages and drive them absurdly low -- to levels that would keep a worker from feeding his family with a day's work.

Because Steinbeck's laborers are unorganized and do not communicate with one another about acceptable pay, they are often powerless against the owners, who also have the benefit of a compliant police force. Conversations among the disgruntled workers are the basis of what the police and owners call "talkin' red," or promoting communism and the power of the proletariat.

> *"Those folks in the camp are getting used to being treated like humans. When they go back to the squatters' camps they'll be hard to handle."*
>
> *Thomas, p. 380*

The farm owners and bosses are unsettled by the conditions that the workers have become accustomed to in the government camps. They realize that they are toeing a fine line between extracting maximum profits and forestalling potential unrest. Just as at other points of the novel, when the intensity of complaints becomes more prominent as people meet one another and interact, here the social life of the workers is creating in them a sense of mutual agitation. One discontented man does not pose a problem, but many disgruntled men, who are living together in a large group, pose a substantial problem to landowners.

Under the capitalism described in *The Grapes of Wrath*, owners' high profit margins rely on the internal competition among laborers that drives wages down. However, if workers decide to strike and not work for certain wages, then the entire corporate system is threatened. Beyond attaining reasonable wage negotiation, the people in the government camp have been able to achieve a certain level of dignity and self-respect. The camp is clean, the residents elect their own officials, and they also work together to provide a better life for everyone. Now that the migrants are experienced in this style of living, the owners fear that the continuation of these living conditions will lead to unrest. Consequently, the owners want to terminate these camps in an attempt to prevent rebellion.

> *"And now the great owners and the companies invented a new method. A great owner bought a cannery. And when the peaches and the pears were ripe he cut the price of fruit below the cost of raising it. And as cannery owner he paid himself a low price for the fruit and kept the price of canned goods up and took his profit. And the little farmers who owned no canneries lost their farms, and they were taken by the great owners, the banks, and the companies who also owned the canneries. As time went on, there were fewer farms. The little farmers moved into town for a while and exhausted their credit, exhausted their friends, their relatives. And then they too went on the highways. And the roads were crowded with men ravenous for work, murderous for work.*
>
> *And the companies, the banks worked at their own doom and they did not know it. The fields were fruitful, and starving men moved on the roads. The granaries were full and the children of the poor grew up rachitic, and the pustules of pellagra swelled on their sides. The great companies did not know that the line between hunger and anger is a thin line. And money that might have gone to wages went for gas, for guns, for agents and spies, for blacklists, for drilling. On the highways the people moved like ants and searched for work, for food. And the anger began to ferment."*

Narrator, p. 364 - 365

The "new method" mentioned above has placed California small farmers in competition with the Okies. Once able to earn a living from their land, the California farmers have been pushed off by larger industrial conglomerates, and now they are traveling up and down California looking for work, just as the people who came from Oklahoma are.

Defined precisely, the "new method" described is a simultaneous process of vertical and horizontal integration.Vertical integration is when the supply chain of a company is owned by the same company. The vertical integration began first: the wealthy owner was able to buy a cannery, use this business to package his goods, and then sell the canned goods to consumers. He was also able to sell his fruit for a relatively high profit because he had control over the prices of the canned goods, since he owned the cannery. Having control over the price of fruit sold to factories allowed the wealthy owner to expand horizontally and push small farmers off their land. The horizontal integration entailed the expansion of one owner across an industry, such as peach production. When both of these processes emerged, it would become impossible for a moderate- or small-sized farm to compete or even continue to exist.

> *"Fella tol' me what happened in Akron, Ohio. Rubber companies. They got mountain people in 'cause they'd work cheap. An' these here mountain people up an' joined the union. Well, sir, hell jes' popped. All them storekeepers and legioners an' people like that, they get drillin' an yellin', 'Red!' An' they're gonna run the union right outa Akron. Preachers git a-preachin' about it, an' papers a-yowlin', an' they're a-buyin' gas. Jesus, you'd think them mountain boys was reg'lar deviles!" He stopped and found some more rocks to shoot. "Well, sir -- it was las' March, an' one Sunday five thousan' of them mountain men had a turkey shoot outside a town. Five thousan' of 'em jes' marched through town with their rifles. An' they had their turkey shoot, an' then they marched back. An' that's all they done. Well, sir, they ain't been no trouble sence then. These here citizens committees give back the pick handles, an' the storekeepers keep their stores, an' nobody been clubbed or tarred an' feathered, an' nobody been killed.' There was a long silence, and then Black Hat said, 'They're gettin purty mean out here. Burned that camp an' beat up folks. I been thinkin'. All our folks got guns. I been thinkin' maybe we ought to git up a turkey shootin' club an' have meetin's ever' Sunday."*
>
> *Black Hat, p. 443 - 444*

When Pa Joad meets with a group of Central Committee members in the government camp, the men's talk turns to quality of life, wages, and work opportunities. A man in a black hat tells the story of a group of people in Akron, Ohio, who fought against the state's powerful rubber companies, suggesting that comparable action could be taken against agricultural giants. The mountain people were also forced to work for lower wages, and when they organized it caused a lot of controversy in their territory. An entire town wanted to break down their organization and run them out -- and the townspeople acquired weapons in order to do so.

The events described in these stories parallel what has been happening in California. People are afraid of organizing because there is little understanding of what it is or what it seeks to accomplish. Yet in a calm show of force -- a march through town, equipped with guns for a "turkey shoot" -- the mountain men were able to establish themselves and prevent actual violence. The man in the black hat suggests that the men in California could do something similar. After all, they all have guns and would be capable of staging a "turkey shoot," and could both assert their strength and organize proactively under this pretext. Because it is impossible for the workers to thrive in the current environment, something drastic must be done to create a better life.

> *"There is a crime here that goes beyond denunciation. There is a sorrow here that weeping cannot symbolize. There is a failure here that topples*

all our success. The fertile earth, the straight tree rows, the sturdy trunks, and the ripe fruit. And children dying of pellagra must die because a profit cannot be taken from an orange. And coroners must fill in the certificates -- died of malnutrition -- because the food must rot, must be forced to rot.

The people come with nets to fish for potatoes in the river, and the guards hold them back; they come in rattling cars to get the dumped oranges, but the kerosene is sprayed. And they stand still and watch the potatoes float by, listen to the screaming pigs being killed in a ditch and covered with quicklime, watch the mountains of oranges slop down to a putrefying ooze; and in the eyes of the hungry there is a growing wrath. In the souls of people the grapes of wrath are filling and growing heavy, growing heavy for the vintage."

Narrator, p. 449

It is in this passage that the title of the novel, *The Grapes of Wrath*, is first mentioned in the text. Understanding the title's origins is important for understanding the larger themes of corporate greed and suffering that are present throughout the novel. The title of the novel can be traced to both the "Battle Hymn of the Republic" and the Bible's Book of Revelation 14: 19-20.

The lyrics of the "Battle Hymn of the Republic" are as follows:

Mine eyes have seen the glory of the coming of the Lord:

He is trampling out the vintage where the grapes of wrath are stored;

He hath loosed the fateful lightning of His terrible swift sword:

His truth is marching on.

(Chorus)

Glory, glory, hallelujah!

Glory, glory, hallelujah!

Glory, glory, hallelujah!

His truth is marching on.

The passage from the Book of Revelation is as follows:

So the angel swung his sickle to the earth and gathered the clusters from the vine of the earth, and threw them into the great wine press of the wrath of God.

The idea of "grapes of wrath" has historically been used to represent the oppression of the weak by the mighty, which occurs throughout the novel as the rich landowners create a miserable existence for the landless laborers. Contained within the phrase is the idea that the anger and wrath of the oppressed becomes deeper and more intense, just as the grapes used to make wine ferment and acquire stronger tastes. In both the "Battle Hymn of the Republic" and the passage from the Book of Revelation, there is a call for a higher power to set right the wrongs that have been done to the oppressed. It is unclear whether Steinbeck is making a plea to God or to some other higher force in the novel. However it is interpreted, this crucial quote places the novel's themes of greed, oppression, suffering, and justice in the context of older, hallowed texts.

The Grapes of Wrath Chapters 1-5 Summary and Analysis

Chapter One: Steinbeck begins the novel with a description of the dust bowl climate of Oklahoma. The dust has become so thick that men and women are forced remain in their houses, and when they are required to leave they tie handkerchiefs over their faces and wear goggles to protect their eyes. After the wind has stopped, an even blanket of dust covers the earth. The corn crop is ruined. Everybody wonders what they should do. Yet the women and children know that no misfortune would be too great to bear if their men were whole, but the men themselves have not yet figured out what to do.

Analysis:

Steinbeck begins the novel with omens of the hardships to come. He describes the arrival of the dust in terms befitting a biblical plague. The dust storm overwhelms Oklahoma, clouding the air and even blocking out the sun. However, the end of the storm only represents the beginning of the hardships for the Oklahoma farmers. A sense of hopelessness sets in almost immediately. There seems to be no solution for the farmers, who are resigned to their fate and find themselves baffled at what they may have to face.

This chapter deliberately does not deal with the characters who will occupy the primary places in the novel, for Steinbeck intends to place his narrative within a larger context. Tom Joad and his family, who will be the focus of *The Grapes of Wrath*, are not yet featured; they make up merely one of thousands of families affected by the events of the Depression. The first chapter serves to give the novel an epic sweep and to remind the reader that the book has a strong historical basis.

Chapter Two: A man approaches a small diner where a large red transport truck is parked. The man is under thirty, with dark brown eyes and high cheekbones. He wears new clothes that don't quite fit. The truck driver exits the diner and the man asks him for a ride, despite the "No Riders" sticker on the truck. The man claims that sometimes a guy will do a good thing even when a rich bastard makes him carry a sticker, and the driver, feeling trapped by the statement, lets the man have a ride. While driving, the truck driver asks questions, and the man finally gives his name, Tom Joad. The truck driver claims that guys do strange things when they drive trucks, such as make up poetry, because of the loneliness of the job. The truck driver also claims that his experience driving has trained his memory and that he can remember everything about a person he comes across. Realizing that the truck driver is trying to glean information, Tom finally admits that he has just been released from McAlester prison, where he had been serving time for homicide. He had been sentenced to seven years and was released after only four, on account of good behavior.

Analysis:

The Oklahoma City Transport Company truck is both imposing and intrusive, a symbol of pervasive corporate influence (as shown by the "No Riders" sticker that is so prominently displayed). Tom Joad immediately voices the idea that business is cold and heartless when he asks the truck driver for a ride. Overall, *The Grapes of Wrath* is unsparingly critical of business and the rich: these groups, here, serve only to keep truck drivers isolated and bored to the point of near insanity.

As for Steinbeck's first primary character, there are several indications that Tom Joad has recently been released from prison. His clothing is recently prison-issued: it does not quite fit him, it is far too formal, and it is spotless so far. He has few possessions with him. The truck driver immediately realizes Tom's recent circumstances; his probing questions, as Tom realizes, are meant to elicit a more particular confession of the crime Tom committed. The little information that Tom reveals about himself shows him to be a shrewd but uneducated man. He can barely write and is accustomed to little more than hard labor, but he is clever enough to know how to manipulate the truck driver into giving him a ride.

A persistent strain of anti-elitism runs throughout the novel. Beyond the contempt that Tom and the truck driver collectively show for big business and the rich, these two men also sharply criticize those who use Œbig words. According to them, only a preacher can use educated language, for a preacher can be trusted. When employed by others, big words merely serve as a means to obscure and confuse.

Chapter Three:

At the side of the road, a turtle crawls, dragging its shell over the grass. This animal comes to the road embankment and, with great effort, climbs onto the road. As the turtle attempts to cross the road, it is nearly hit by a sedan. A truck swerves to hit the turtle, but its wheel only strikes the edge of the turtle's shell and spins the turtle back off the highway. The turtle finds itself on its back, but finally sets itself right.

Analysis:

The turtle is a symbol of the working class farmers whose stories and struggles are recounted in *The Grapes of Wrath.* The turtle plods along dutifully, but is consistently confronted with danger and setbacks. Significantly, the dangers posed to the turtle are those of modernity and business: the intrusion of cars and the building of highways both endanger the turtle. The truck that strikes this creature is a symbol of big business and commerce. The Joad family -- which will soon be introduced in its entirety -- will experience travails analogous to those of the turtle as the family members plod along, wishing only to survive yet brutally pushed aside by corporate interests.

Chapter Four: After getting out of the truck, Tom Joad begins walking home. He sees the turtle that appeared in the previous chapter and picks it up. He stops in the shade of a tree to rest and finds a man sitting there and singing "Jesus Is My Savior."

The man, Jim Casy, has a long, bony frame and sharp features. A former minister, Casy recognizes Tom immediately. Casy was a "Burning Busher" who used to "howl out the name of Jesus to glory," but he abandoned his calling because he found that too many sinful ideas seemed sensible. Tom tells Casy that he took the turtle for his little brother, and Casy replies that nobody can keep a turtle, for eventually the turtle will wander off on its own. Casy claims that he doesn't know where he's going now; Tom tells him to lead people, even if he doesn't know where to lead them. Casy tells Tom that part of the reason he quit preaching was that he too often succumbed to temptation, having sex with many of the girls he Œsaved. Finally, he realized that perhaps what he was doing wasn't a sin; perhaps, according to Casy, there isn't really sin or virtue, simply things that people do.

Tom tells Casy why he was in jail: he was at a dance, got drunk, and got into a fight with another man. The man cut Tom with a knife, so Tom hit the man over the head with a shovel. Tom then informs Casy that he was treated relatively well in McAlester. He ate regularly, got clean clothes, and was able to bathe. He even states that another prisoner broke his parole in order to go back. Tom also relates a little Joad family history and tells how his father Œstole the family house. The former residents of the house had moved away, so Tom's father, uncle, and grandfather cut the house in two and dragged half of it away, although a man named Wink Manley took the other half. Soon enough, Tom and Casy arrive at the boundary fence of the Joads' property; the Joads didn't need a fence, but having one gave Pa a feeling that the family's forty acres was forty acres. Upon reaching the house, Tom and Casy find that something odd has happened. Nobody is there.

Analysis:

Jim Casy is the moral voice of the novel and its religious center. He is a religious icon, a philosopher and a prophet. His initials (J.C.) reveal that Steinbeck has designed him as a Christ figure; in fact, he espouses Steinbeck's interpretation of religious doctrine. Casy eschews dogma and scripture, even any semblance of a strict moral code. Instead, Casy finds the rules and regulations of Christian teachings severely confining and clearly inapplicable to actual situations. The most striking case of this is his history of sexual activity with the women he converts. Casy originally felt tremendously guilty over his actions and worried about his responsibilities toward the women he was trying to direct to Jesus, yet finally came to the conclusion that "maybe it's just the way folks is." Casy's final more code resists solid definition. He denies the existence of virtue or vice, finding that "there's just stuff people do. It's all part of the same thing." His final conclusion is that all men and women are the Holy Spirit, connected by one common soul.

Steinbeck thus focuses on the common people not only politically (for instance, by playing up the theme of poverty during the Great Depression) but also religiously. Casy rejects the idea of Jesus as intangible: he does not and cannot know Jesus, but he does know common people and believes them to be the representation of God. Even Tom's stories demonstrate a dislike of concrete religious structure. He mocks the pious religious Christmas card that his grandmother sent him while he was in prison.

Tom's description of the prison demonstrates the poverty under which he and his family struggle. For Tom, living in prison ensured that he would be fed and cared for. Now that he has re-entered society, he has no such guarantees. The story of how Tom's family obtained their house further demonstrates his family's desperation to establish property and security; they were forced to literally take their home from someone else. Yet Tom tells Casy all this in the form of a humorous anecdote. Poverty has become so ingrained that all that Tom can do is accept it.

Chapter Five: This chapter describes the coming of the bank representatives to evict the farmers. Some of the representatives are kind because they knew how cruel their job is, yet some are angry because they hate to be cruel, while yet others are merely cold and hardened by their job. These men are mostly pawns of a larger system and have no choice but to obey. For its part, the tenant system has become untenable for the banks, since one man on a tractor can efficiently take the place of a dozen families. The farmers raise the possibility of armed insurrection, but what would they fight against? They will be murderers if they stay, fighting against the wrong targets -- the messengers of the banks, not the banks themselves.

Steinbeck describes the arrival of the tractors. They crawl over the ground, cutting the earth like surgeons and violating it like rapists. The tractor driver does his job out of simple necessity: he has to feed his kids, even if doing so comes at the expense of dozens of families. To highlight the cruel logic of the entire situation, Steinbeck dramatizes a conversation between a truck driver and an evicted tenant farmer. The farmer threatens to kill the driver, but such violence would accomplish nothing. Another driver will come. Even if the farmer murders the president of the bank and board of directors, the bank is controlled by people from the East. There is no effective target which could be destroyed in a way that would prevent the evictions.

Analysis:

Even more than the coming of the dust, the arrival of the bankers is an ominous event. For Steinbeck, the banks have no redeeming value. They are completely devoid of human characteristics: they are monstrosities that "breathe profits" and can never be satiated. Steinbeck explicitly states that a bank is inhuman, and that the bank owner with fifty thousand acres is a "monster." A bank is made by men but is something more than and separate from people, a destructive force that pursues short-term profits at the expense of the land, destroying the landscape through cotton production that drains the terrain of its resources.

Steinbeck describes the movement of the tractors over the ground as indiscriminate and hostile. The tractors move arbitrarily, violently slicing the ground with their blades. Steinbeck first equates the plowing with surgery, but goes further to compare it to a rape: a cold and passionless intrusion into the land, and an event unconnected with human emotion.

According to Steinbeck, personal connection to the land determines ownership. A man who does not reside on his land and walk upon it cannot own it; rather, the property controls the man and he becomes the servant of the land.

In this critique of the banks, the behavior of the employees is largely excusable. They are "caught in something larger than themselves," controlled by the mathematics of bank operations and slaves to the company that has ensnared them. The situation that the bank poses for the farmers leaves them no options. They cannot defend the land, for they would be murdering men who are not genuinely responsible for the land's fate. They can only leave. The tractor drivers face a similar situation. Despite the suffering of the farmers, they have to work somehow to feed their families. They are not responsible for what they do, for they are controlled by larger forces.

The conversation between the tenant farmer and the tractor driver illustrates how far-reaching the controlling corporate system is. If a farmer were to attempt to stop the bank, he could not do so by targeting one individual or even a small group; even if a farmer murdered the bank president, such a murder would not stop the process of evictions. The people are helpless.

The Grapes of Wrath Chapters 6-9 Summary and Analysis

Chapter Six:

Casy and Tom approach the Joad home. The house has been mashed in at one corner and is apparently deserted. Casy says that it looks like the arm of the Lord has struck. Tom can tell that Ma isn't there, for she would have never left the gate in its present, unhooked state. The two men only see one resident (the cat), but Tom wonders why the cat hasn't gone to find another family if his family has moved and wonders further why the neighbors haven't taken the belongings that remain in the house.

Muley Graves -- a short, lean old man with the truculent look of an ornery child -- approaches Tom and Casy. Muley tells Tom that his family was evicted and had to move in with his Uncle John. The Joads were forced to chop cotton to make enough money to go west in search of better conditions. Muley also tells Tom and Casy that the loss of the farmland broke up his own family: Muley's wife and kids went off to California, yet Muley chose to stay. In his present state of deprivation, he has been forced to eat wild game. He muses about how angry he was when he was told he had to get off the land. First he wanted to kill people, but then his family set off and Muley was left alone to wander. He realizes that he has become accustomed to his new lifestyle, even if he must roam the land like a ghost.

Tom tells Muley and Casy that he can't go to California, as many of the tenants have, for it would mean breaking his parole. Prison has not changed Tom significantly, in Tom's own opinion. He thinks that if he saw Herb Turnbull, the man he killed, coming after him with a knife again, he would still hit him with the shovel. Tom tells his companions that there was a man in McAlester who read a great deal about prisons and who told him that they started a long time ago and now cannot be stopped, despite the fact that they do not actually rehabilitate people. As the conversation winds down, Muley tells his companions that they have to hide, for they are trespassing on the land. The three hide in a cave for the night.

Analysis:

When Tom and Casy return to the Joad home, it appears foreign and unfriendly. The house is empty, but for Tom the situation is unnatural. There are signs that the family has left, but suspiciously everyone else seems to have left as well.

Muley Graves echoes the previous chapter's idea that no matter whom a man might kill, the banks cannot be stopped. Eventually, Muley enters a state of resignation, forced to accept his fate. The character is essentially a ghost, living on the outskirts of society and wandering the land, bereft of his wife and children. His fate demonstrates the dehumanizing quality of the banks' intrusions: he is a man without any impetus to participate in life.

In telling Muley and Casy that he has not been rehabilitated by his jail term, Tom effectively issues a warning that, despite his calm demeanor, he is still a man capable of violence. This foreshadows later developments; if Tom is provoked, there is still the possibility that he could react viciously. Neither Tom nor Muley believes in the rehabilitating power of prisons. According to Muley, the only type of government force that can manipulate human behavior is the capitalist system, the idea of the Œsafe "margin of profit." Muley's belief reinforces Steinbeck's depiction of the corporate system as the real controlling force in society, more powerful than any citizen or group of citizens yet without concern for them.

Even spending the night on abandoned property places Tom, Casy, and Muley in danger. They are trespassing, and must hide in a cave in order to protect themselves from patrolling deputies. Muley makes an apt comparison between the men and hunted animals, forced into subterfuge and unable to even show themselves in the open.

Chapter Seven: The car dealership owners look at their customers. They watch for weak and easily manipulated visitors, such as a woman who wants an expensive car and can push her husband to buy one. They attempt to make the customers feel obliged. Yet the true profits come from selling jalopies, not from selling new and dependable cars. There are no guarantees, only hidden costs and obvious flaws.

Analysis:

This chapter critiques yet another part of the business system. The owners of the car dealerships mean solely to exploit impoverished buyers. They do not profit from selling cars that will last, but rather from finding the most ill-used vehicle, giving it the appearance of reliability, and selling it off to desperate farmers who want to get to California. There is no compassion in the market for cars, just a perpetual cycle of exploitation. This chapter indicates what the Joad family must certainly have experienced to obtain a car before going west, yet places the family's experiences in a larger context.

Chapter Eight: Tom and Casy reach Uncle John's farm. They remark that Muley's lonely and furtive lifestyle has obviously driven him insane. According to Tom, the Joads' Uncle John is equally crazy; this relative wasn't expected to live long yet is older than Tom's father. Still, Uncle John is astonishingly tough and mean, hardened by losing his young wife years ago. Tom and Casy see Pa Joad fixing the family's truck. When Pa sees Tom, he assumes that Tom broke out of jail. The men go into the house and see Ma Joad, a heavy woman thick with child-bearing and constant work. Her face is controlled and kindly.

This chapter also introduces Grampa and Granma Joad, as well as a few other Joad relatives. Granma is as tough as Grampa is, and once shot her husband while she was speaking in tongues. Noah Joad, Tom's older brother, is a strange man, slow and withdrawn, with little pride and few urges. (He may have experienced brain damage during his infancy.) The family has dinner and Casy says grace. He talks about how Jesus went off into the wilderness alone, and how he did the same, ultimately arriving at the conclusion that mankind is holy. Pa tells Tom about Al, Tom's sixteen-year old brother, who is concerned with little more than girls and cars. He hasn't been at home at night for a week. Furthermore, Tom's sister Rosasharn has married Connie Rivers and is several months pregnant. In terms of resources, the family has two hundred dollars at its disposal for the coming journey west.

Analysis:

The members of the Joad family are tough and unrefined people, hardened by their experiences. Uncle John has gone nearly mad from losing his wife to illness, Pa Joad is sullen and withdrawn, and Grampa is too angry and bitter to even stay in the house. Only Ma Joad retains some level of warmth and compassion. She worries that Tom might have gone insane in prison. However, even she has changed, as Tom remarks, for until recently she had never had her house pushed over and had never had to sell everything she owned. Even Granma Joad is a mean, weathered woman.

Despite some of these unappealing family traits, Casy's speech at dinner is yet another example of Steinbeck's glorification of the common person. For Casy and Steinbeck alike, the population as a whole exemplifies what is holy. It is only when people diverge from the common good that they become unholy. This theme is also evident in Ma Joad's musings that there might be hope if everybody became angry enough to rise up against the moneyed powers. Steinbeck takes a largely socialistic viewpoint here, championing the common good over individual interests.

Chapter Nine: This chapter describes the process of selling belongings. The items pile up in yards, selling for ridiculously low prices. Whatever is not sold must be burned, even items of sentimental value that simply cannot be taken on the journey for lack of space.

Analysis:

The sale of the items is a demeaning process, for the farmers must accept ridiculously low prices for their now-useless possessions. Steinbeck is explicit about the meaning of the sales: he states that "you're not buying only junk, you're buying junked lives." This is yet another example of the dehumanizing effects of the Depression foreclosures. The situation is hopeless: there is no possibility of starting over, because the people who are leaving are now imbued with bitterness and loss. They must even give up out of simple necessity those objects that have sentimental value -- yet another example of the loss of human individuality and personal attachment.

The Grapes of Wrath Chapters 10-13 Summary and Analysis

Chapter Ten:

Ma Joad tells Tom that she is concerned about going to California, worried that it won't turn out well, for the only information the family has gleaned is from flyers. Despite these reservations, Casy asks to accompany the Joads to California. He wants to work in the fields, where he can listen to people rather than preach to them. Tom says that preaching is a tone of voice and a style, being good to people when they don't respond to it. Pa and Uncle John greet the rest of the family with the truck, and they all prepare to leave. The two young children, twelve-year old Ruthie and ten-year old Winfield, are there with their older sister, Rose of Sharon (Rosasharn) and her husband.

That night, the Joads hold a family conference and discuss a number of issues: they decide to allow Casy to come along with them, since it's the right thing for them to do. They also continue with their preparations, killing their pigs so that they will have food to take with them. While Casy is helping Ma Joad with food preparation, he remarks that she looks tired, perhaps sick. Ma Joad looks through her belongings, going through old letters and clippings she has saved; she burns these items before the family's departure. Before the Joads leave, Muley Graves stops in to say goodbye. Noah tells him that he's going to die out in the fields if he stays, but Muley accepts his fate. In another case of attachment to the land, Grampa refuses to leave; the other Joads decide to give him medicine that knocks him out and manage to take him with them.

Analysis:

This chapter illustrates the Joad family dynamic. The presence of numerous relatives from across three generations makes maintaining order difficult, as the family meeting demonstrates. The Joad family has Grampa as its nominal head, yet he exerts no special influence. If any member of the family leads the others, it is Ma Joad, who dominates by moral force. It is she who issues the final verdict that allows Casy to go with them to California. While Tom Joad is the main character in *The Grapes of Wrath*, Ma Joad is the story's moral center, reminding everyone that they have greater concerns than just their own interests. As she indicates, it would be wrong of them to refuse food or shelter to anyone.

Yet Ma Joad appears to be the principal victim of the move to California. Casy notices that she looks ill from recent events, and she is the only one in the family who appears to have regrets. For the others, this is surely an unfortunate move, yet Ma Joad must leave behind the memories that she treasures. Even Grampa, when he refuses to leave, does so in a display of bitter energy. Ma Joad, in contrast, is overcome with a great weariness.

Grampa's refusal to leave highlights how important the land is for the Joads and for other people like them. For Grampa, leaving the area where he was born and raised is unimaginable. Yet he has no options. If he were to remain, he would essentially cease to exist, much like Muley Graves.

Chapter Eleven:

The houses have been left vacant. Only the tractor sheds made of gleaming iron and silver are alive. Yet when the tractors are at rest the life goes out of them. The work of these machines is easy and efficient, so easy that the wonder goes out of the work and so efficient that the wonder goes out of the land and its cultivation. In the tractor, a man grows a spirit of contempt, since such a man is a stranger who has little understanding of and no relation to the land. The abandoned houses slowly fall apart.

Analysis:

This chapter provides one more critique of the new means of cotton production that is overtaking the farms. The fate of the tractors contrasts sharply with that of the farmers who once worked there. The tractors and their drivers have no connection to the land, little understanding of and no relationship with it. The farmers, in contrast, have a deep and long-standing affection for the land on which they lived and worked; this is part of the reason why Grampa, in the previous chapter, refused to leave Oklahoma.

Steinbeck also continues to remind the reader that the tractors are inhuman. He creates a mocking metaphor (in which the tractors Œgo home at the end of the day and Œgo to sleep) to demonstrate how far the spectacle of the tractors is from an actual human experience. Steinbeck even explicitly establishes how "dead" the tractors are, comparing one to a corpse.

Chapter Twelve: Highway 66 is the main migrant road stretching from the Mississippi River to Bakersfield, California. It is a road of flight for refugees from dust and poverty. The people stream out onto Highway 66, risking the breakdown of their undependable cars on the way. And the travelers face other obstacles. California is a big state, but not big enough to support all of the workers who are approaching The border patrol can turn people back. The high wages that are promised may be a deception.

Analysis:

In this chapter, Steinbeck foreshadows a number of the problems that the Joad family will face on its travels. He highlights the problems that people often have with their cars -- including the possibility of breakdown, a problem that may afflict the Joad family's unreliable vehicle.

Building off earlier segments of *The Grapes of Wrath*, this chapter begins to affirm the unpleasant fact that California may not be a panacea for the Joads' problems. Even if the Joads reach the California border, they may be turned back. So many others are making the same journey that there is bound to be an overcrowded job market among the migrant workers in California. Arrival in California does not necessarily mean that the Joads' problems will be solved or that they will be in even a marginally better situation than faced them in Oklahoma.

Chapter Thirteen:

The Joads continue on their travels. Al remarks that they may have trouble getting over mountains in their car, which can barely support the weight of the family and its belongings. Grampa Joad wakes up and insists that he's not going with the rest of the Joads. They stop at a gas station where the owner automatically assumes they are broke and tells them that people often stop, begging for gas.

The owner claims that fifty cars per day go west, but wonders what the Joads expect to find when they reach their destination. He tells that one family traded their daughter's doll for some gas. Casy wonders what the nation is coming to, since people seem unable to make a decent living; he says that he once had used his energy to fight the devil, believing that the devil was the enemy. However, now he believes that there's something worse.

The Joad's dog wanders away from the car and is run over in the road. The family members continue on their journey and begin to worry when they reach the state line. However, Tom reassures them that he is only in danger if he commits a crime. Otherwise, nobody will know that he has broken his parole by leaving his home state. On their next stop for the night, the Joads meet the Wilsons, a family from Kansas that is going to California. Grampa complains of illness and weeps, causing the rest of the family to fear that he will suffer a stroke. Granma tells Casy to pray for Grampa, even if he is no longer a preacher. Suddenly Grampa starts twitching and slumps; he dies abruptly. The Joads now face a choice: they can pay fifty dollars for a proper burial for Grampa or have him buried as a pauper. They decide to bury Grampa themselves and leave a note so that people don't assume that he was murdered. In a show of solidarity, the Wilsons help the Joads to bury Grampa. A verse from scripture is included in the note on his grave.

After burying Grampa, the Joads have Casy say a few words. Overall, the reactions to the death are varied. Rose of Sharon comforts Granma, while Uncle John is curiously unmoved by the turn of events. Casy admits that he knew Grampa was dying, but didn't say anything because he couldn't have helped. He blames separation from the land for Grampa's death. Yet the Joads are given assistance during this difficult time: the Joads and the Wilsons decide to help each other by distributing weight between their two cars so that both families will make it to California.

Analysis:

The first stop that the Joads make reinforces the idea that they may not find work when they reach California because of a glutted labor market. But even when confronted with a dire situation, the Joads are nevertheless better off than some travelers; at the very least, the Joads are able to pay for gas.

Casy reiterates the idea that the nation faces a nearly unconquerable enemy. Although he does not explicitly identify this enemy, its characteristics indicate that it is the capitalist system that was vilified earlier in the novel. Casy depicts the enemy as a system that prevents normal people from making a decent living. For Casy, this Œevil is too powerful to effectively combat -- more daunting and more difficult to oppose than even the devil.

Early in the journey the Joads suffer a fateful loss, if one less significant than the loss of an actual family member -- the death of the family dog. Its early demise, which occurs before the Joads even reach the Oklahoma border, foreshadows the further losses that the family may suffer. Steinbeck further anticipates the problems that the Joads may face when Tom mentions parole violations. He is only in danger if he commits another crime, yet his difficult temperament keeps that danger alive.

The death of the dog is followed by the death of an actual family member. Despite his tough veneer of anger and bitterness, Grampa is in fact sensitive to the family's uprooting. Since he was the one family member most adamantly opposed to leaving home, it is likely the separation that hastened his demise. Casy makes a direct correlation between Grampa's death and the Joads' journey, reinforcing the idea that these people have a significant personal connection the the land they farmed.

Throughout the novel, Casy frequently must perform the duties of a preacher. Although he maintains that he no longer believes in preaching, he is forced to perform his old role, whether praying for Grampa during the stroke or saying a few parting words after Grampa's burial. This seems to indicate that Casy is ideally suited for the role of preacher, despite his disenchantment with religion. In his parting words for Grampa Joad, Casy does reiterate his belief that people are the source of holiness.

The agreement between the Joads and the Wilsons to aid each other on the way to California is a significant plot development, for it is in collective action that these families find their strength. This cooperation is the first building block in a collectivist scheme that Steinbeck seems to support -- a scheme in which working class people come together to improve their mutual lot in life.

The Grapes of Wrath Chapters 14-17 Summary and Analysis

Chapter Fourteen: The Western States are nervous about several new factors, including widening government influence, growing labor unity, and strikes. However, these states do not realize that these factors are results of change and not causes of it. The true cause is the hunger of the multitude. The danger that established powers face is that the people's perspective on social problems has moved from "I" to "we."

Analysis:

This chapter makes an explicit political statement concerning the migration to the west coast. The owners and controlling powers fear the changes that are imminent and that threaten their interests. However, the owners are the cause of such changes. By forcing the farmers from their land, business interests have created the hunger that afflicts the farmers.

Steinbeck once again considers the definition and function of a man. According to him, a man is defined by what he creates, what work he does, and -- most importantly -- his ability for improvement. The narration warns against the prospect of mankind ceasing to struggle for improvement, even though that struggle leads to sacrifice. This chapter is an attempt to create a larger perspective on mankind as something greater than the collective interest of individuals. According to Steinbeck, mankind is distinguished because men's actions can go beyond the individual man.

This chapter also pinpoints the adversarial relationship between the owners and the working classes. The owners exploit individual interests in order to thwart the collective good. By forcing men to consider only self-interest, the owners prevent the possibility that collective interest may form and foment revolution.

Chapter Fifteen: This chapter begins with a description of the hamburger stands and diners on Route 66. The typical diner is run by an often-irritated woman, who nevertheless becomes friendly when truck drivers -- consistent customers who can always pay -- enter. The more wealthy travelers drop names and buy vanity products. The owners of the diners complain about the migrating workers, who can't pay and often steal. A family comes into a designated diner, wanting to buy a loaf of bread. The one owner, Mae, tells them that her business is not a grocery store, but Al, the other, is more receptive. For her part, Mae eventually sells the family candy for reduced prices. Mae and Al wonder what such families will do once they reach California.

Analysis:

Instead of depicting the plight of the migrant families from the perspective of the Joads, this chapter gives another, somewhat unsympathetic perspective on the migrants' situation. For the people who own the diners and other small businesses along Route 66, the migrant workers are little more than a burden, since the migrants ask these people, who are simply attempting to make a living, for handouts and charity. The men and women who work at the diners on Route 66 view the migrant families with a conflicted sense of loathing and compassion. They see these travelers as shiftless and threatening, yet do take pity on them. Mae and Al sell one group of migrants a loaf of bread and Mae even sells the children candy for a much-reduced price. Yet part of this compassion stems from impatience. It is easier to give the migrant families what they want and send them on their way.

Chapter Sixteen: The Joads and the Wilsons continue on their travels. Rose of Sharon discusses with her mother what they will do when they reach California. She and Connie want to live in a town, where Connie can get a job in a store or a factory. He also wants to study at home, possibly taking a radio correspondence course. Then there is a rattling in the Wilson's car, so Al is forced to pull over; it turns out that there are problems with the motor.

Sairy Wilson tells the Joads that they should go ahead without the Wilsons, but Ma Joad refuses, telling them that they are like family now and that the group won't desert its members. Tom says that he and Casy will stay with the truck if everyone else goes on ahead; they'll fix the car and then move on. However, Ma objects. She refuses to go, for the only thing that the migrants have left is each other and she will not break up the family even momentarily. When everyone else objects to her argument, she picks up a jack handle and threatens them.

Tom and Casy try to fix the car, and Casy remarks that he has seen so many cars moving west, but no cars going east. Casy predicts that all of the movement and collection of people in California will change the country. The two of them stay with the car while the family goes ahead. Before the bulk of the family leaves, Al tells Tom that Ma is worried that he will do something that might break his parole. And this is not the only cause for concern: Granma has been going crazy, yelling and talking to herself. Al asks Tom about what he felt when he killed a man. Tom admits that prison has a tendency to drive a man insane.

Tom and Al find a junkyard, where they locate a replacement part for the broken con-rod in the Wilsons' car. The one-eyed man working at the junkyard complains about his boss, and says that he might kill him. Tom tells off the one-eyed man for blaming all of his problems on his eye, and then criticizes Al for his constant worry that people will blame him for the car breaking down. Soon enough, Tom, Casy, and Al rejoin the rest of the family at a campground not far away. Yet to stay at the campground, the three are required to pay an additional charge, for they would be charged with vagrancy if they slept out in the open. Tom, Casy, and Uncle John eventually decide to go on ahead and meet up with everyone else in the morning.

The Joads also learn more about their California prospects. A ragged man at the camp, when he hears that the Joads are going to pick oranges in California, laughs.

The man, who is returning from California, declares that the handbills are fraudulent: the handbills demand eight hundred people, but attract several thousand people who want to work. This drives down wages. The proprietor of the campground suspects that the ragged man is trying to stir up trouble.

Analysis:

Rose of Sharon offers a stark contrast to the rest of the characters in *The Grapes of Wrath*. She is the only adult character who retains some sense of hope for the Joads' future; she believes in the possibility of living a decent life with her husband and eventual child. While the other characters expect little more from California than meager survival, Rose of Sharon hopes to live the traditional American dream. She is the one beacon of hope within the Joad family. Even her younger brother, Al, does not possess a similar optimism. He is defensive and combative, consistently worried that others will blame him for problems with the car.

Ma Joad once again reveals herself as the center of the Joad family when she demands that the Joads not leave Tom and Casy behind, even temporarily. She leaves the family no option but to remain together, even threatening violence against anybody who opposes her. In doing so, she reiterates the idea that the strength of disadvantaged people such as the Joads depends on unity.

Steinbeck makes it quite clear by the end of the chapter that the Joads might not find work in California. Casy mentions that he has seen numerous others travel westward, but has seen nobody travel back east, and the ragged man that the Joads meet at the campground confirms this fear. Even worse than a crowded labor market is the fact that the presumed opportunities for jobs are deceptions, that the handbills have induced too many workers in order to drive down wages. The ragged man even suggests that the Joads will face a worse fate in California than they did in Oklahoma. For revealing this information, the ragged man is automatically pegged as a labor agitator -- a derisive label consistently given to those who expose social injustices in Steinbeck's novel.

The one-eyed man provides yet another slant on the American experience. He is garish and grotesque, and his introduction is a break from the thorough realism of the novel. The one-eyed man reveals his life story almost immediately -- a device that is far from credibly realistic but serves to give him some psychological layering. He is one of the many workers the Joads encounter, but he is not insignificant. Steinbeck gives him some personality and history to emphasize the importance of all working people, whether or not they occupy central roles in *The Grapes of Wrath*. The episode with the one-eyed man also demonstrates once again that Tom Joad is forthright and direct. He will not shy away from standing up to a person -- a quality that gives him an air of authority but may still prove dangerous.

Chapter Seventeen: An important pattern of behavior emerges among the migrant laborers. During the day, as they travel, their cars are separate and lonely, yet in the evening a strange thing happens: at the campgrounds where they stay the twenty or so families become one. Their losses and their concerns become communal. The families are at first timid, but they gradually build small societies within the campgrounds, with codes of behavior and rights that must be observed. For transgressions, there are only two punishments: violence and ostracism. Leaders emerge, generally the wise elders. The various families find connections to one another

Analysis:

This chapter focuses on the society of the migrant workers, a somewhat idealized society that forms spontaneously. It is an essentially communal society, one with rules and regulations that determine polite behavior and that enable the various, disparate families to find common interests. In essence, Steinbeck uses the campground life to depict a utopian order in which ostentatious displays of wealth are shunned, equality reigns, and no real ruling class emerges. The closest approximation to a ruling class is the group of elders, who rule from wisdom and experience.

The Grapes of Wrath Chapters 18-21 Summary and Analysis

Chapter Eighteen: When the Joads reach Arizona, a border guard stops them and nearly turns them back, but finally lets them continue. They eventually reach the desert of California. The terrain here is barren and desolate. While washing themselves during a stop, the Joads encounter migrant workers who want to turn back; during this encounter, the Joads are informed that the Californians hate the migrant workers. A good deal of the land is owned by the Land and Cattle Company, which leaves the land largely untouched. Sheriffs push around migrant workers and derisively call them "Okies."

Noah tells Tom that he is going to leave everyone, for they don't care about him. Although Tom protests, Noah does depart. Granma remains ill, suffering from delusions. She believes that she sees Grampa. A Jehovite woman visits the Joads' tent to help Granma, and tells Ma that Granma will die soon. The woman also wants to organize a prayer meeting, but Ma orders the woman not to. Nevertheless, soon Ma can hear distant chanting and singing, which eventually descends into crying. Eventually, Granma Joad falls asleep.

Deputies come to the tent and tell Ma that the Joads cannot stay and that the authorities don't want any Okies around. Tom returns to the tent after the police leave, and feels glad that he wasn't there; he admits that he would have hit the cops. He then tells Ma about Noah. The Wilsons decide to remain even if they face arrest, since Sairy is sick and needs more time to recuperate. Sairy asks Casy to say a prayer for her. The Joads move on, and at a stop a boy remarks that Okies are hard-looking and less-than-human. Uncle John, who fears that he brings bad luck, speaks with Casy about this belief. Yet again the Joads are pulled over for inspection, but Ma Joad insists that the family must continue because Granma needs medical attention. The next morning, when the Joads reach the orange groves, Ma tells the rest of her family that Granma is dead. She had died before they were pulled over for inspection.

Analysis:

The arrival in California is anticlimactic at best. The Joads cross the border only to enter the harsh California desert. They still must journey farther to reach the orange groves. There is further evidence that California will not offer a genuine solution to the Joads' problems. The migrant workers are loathed, and there is no way to avoid the difficult conditions created by wealthy corporate interests. The rich owners are characterized as paranoid, vindictive, and cowardly. Steinbeck even creates an explicit contrast between the cowardly owners and Grampa, a fearless old man even in his final days. The rich owners have wealth, but they suffer from loneliness and fear. In this manner, they are worse off than even the most impoverished.

The Joad family loses yet another member once it reaches California, when Noah decides to leave. However, this loss is voluntary, since Noah, Tom's frequently-ignored brother, simply decides that he will stay near a river and support himself by fishing. This loss emphasizes the sense of hopelessness that has set in. Noah, like Muley Graves, decides to leave society instead of being crushed by it.

Although Granma seems to be on the brink of death at the beginning of this chapter, she temporarily pulls through. Once again Ma takes charge, ordering the Jehovites to leave her family alone. She even confronts the deputies who threaten her, effectively intimidating them. The deputies are the first major manifestation of the contempt toward "Okies" that was mentioned earlier in the chapter. Hatred of Okies is made even more explicit by the boy at the gas station, who remarks that the Okies are less than human.

The various members of the Joad family become more tense and irritable as the journey continues. Rose of Sharon and Connie begin to feel a sense of claustrophobia, bothered by the lack of privacy, while Uncle John worries irrationally that he may be the cause of the family's troubles. Uncle John, like Sairy Wilson, wishes to use Casy as a preacher, a designation Casy loathes but nevertheless accepts. Casy's protestations that he is not a preacher and does not believe in God seem excessive. He refuses to be called a preacher because he has doubts, and others approach him expecting that, as a former preacher, he will be a source of certainty.

Perhaps the most dramatic event in this chapter, the death of Granma Joad is significant because it demonstrates just how much Ma Joad can bear -- and how relentless she can be. The event forces her to confront and intimidate several police officers and to hide Granma's fate from the rest of the family.

Chapter Nineteen: California once belonged to Mexico and its land to the Mexicans. But a horde of tattered, feverish Americans poured in and took over the land. As the Americans gained control, farming became a systematic industry. The Americans imported Chinese, Japanese, Mexican and Filipino workers, who essentially served as slaves. The owners of the farms ceased to be farmers and became businessmen; they hated the Okies because they could not profit from this set of arrivals. Other laborers hated the Okies because they pushed down wages. While the native Californians had aspirations to social success and luxury, the barbarous Okies only wanted land and food. Hoovervilles arose at the edges of towns all over the state. And dislike of the Okies took other forms: deputies overreacted to the Okies, spurred by stories that an eleven year-old Okie had shot a deputy. With all this history of tension, the great owners realize that when property accumulates in too few hands it is taken away and that when a majority of the people are hungry and cold they will take by force what they need.

Analysis:

Steinbeck traces what he sees as the sorry history of California, fraught with indignity and oppression. Americans took the land from the Mexicans, placed Asian workers into virtual slavery, and finally condemned the Okies to build shantytowns. Yet Steinbeck predicts that the conclusion of this history will be the overthrow of the capitalist owner class. To some extent, he relies on Marxist-Leninist predictions that capitalist imperialism creates its demise through its own success. Eventually, the accumulation of wealth in too few hands will deprive the population to such a degree that the people will have no choice but to revolt.

Chapter Twenty: The Joads take Granma to the Bakersfield coroner's office, but find that they can't afford a funeral for her. They go to a camp to ask about work; they ask a bearded man if he owns the camp and whether they can stay, and he replies to them with the same question. A younger man tells them that the bearded, crazy old man is called the Mayor. According to this younger man, the Mayor has apparently been pushed around by the police so much that he's been made bull-simple (or crazy). The police don't want Okies to settle down, for then they could draw relief, organize, and vote. The younger man tells the Joads about the handbill fraud, affirming earlier suspicions, and Tom suggests that everybody organize so that they can guarantee higher wages. Upon hearing this, the young man warns Tom about the blacklist. If Tom is labeled an agitator, he will be prevented from getting work from anybody. Tom talks to Casy, who has recently been relatively quiet. Casy says that the people without organization are like an army without a harness. Ultimately, Casy says that he isn't helping the family out and should go off by himself. Tom tries to convince him to stay, at least until the next day, and Casy relents. However, there are other notes of discontent: Connie regrets his decision to come with the Joads. He says that if he had stayed in Oklahoma he could have worked as a tractor driver.

When Ma is fixing dinner, groups of small children approach, asking for food. The children tell the Joads about Weedpatch, a government camp that is nearby, a place where the cops cannot push people around and where there is good drinking water. Al goes around looking for girls, and brags about how Tom killed a man. Al also meets a man named Floyd Knowles, who tells the Joads that there is no steady work. Al brings Floyd back to the family, and Floyd says that there will be work up north, around Santa Clara Valley. He tells the Joads to leave quietly, because everyone else will follow after in search of the work. Al wants to go with Floyd no matter what.

A little later, a man in a business suit arrives in a Chevrolet coupe. He tells the migrants about work picking fruit around Tulare County. Floyd tells the man to show his license; this (appearing without a license) is one of the tricks that the contractors use. Floyd then points out even more of the dirty tactics that the contractor is using, such as bringing along a cop.

The cop forces Floyd into the car and says that the Board of Health might want to shut down the camp. However, Floyd punches the cop and runs off. Tom aids in the escape by tripping the deputy. The deputy raises his gun to shoot Floyd and fires indiscriminately, shooting a woman in the hand. Suddenly, Casy kicks the deputy in the back of the neck, knocking him unconscious. Casy tells Tom to hide, since the contractor saw him trip the deputy. More officers come to the scene, and they take away Casy, who has a faint smile and a look of pride.

After this scene of chaos, the family takes stock of its situation. Rose of Sharon wonders where Connie has gone. She has not seen him recently. Uncle John, for his part, admits that he has five dollars, which he wants to spend on drink. Yet Uncle John now gives the family the five in exchange for two, which is enough money for him. Al tells Rose of Sharon that he saw Connie leaving the area. Pa claims that Connie was too big for his overalls, but Ma scolds him, telling him to act respectfully, as if Connie were dead. Because the cops are going to burn the camp at night, the Joads are forced to leave. Tom goes to find Uncle John, who has gone off to get drunk, and locates him singing morosely beside a river. He claims that he wants to die; because of Uncle John's difficult state, Tom has to hit him to make him come along. Together, the Joads leave the camp, heading north toward the government camp.

Analysis:

The cruelty of the California police is prominent in this chapter, beginning with the introduction of the Mayor. This character has been subjected to continuous torture by the police, a process which has driven him insane. The reason for this torture is simple: such torture is an attempt by the police to prevent the migrant workers from settling in California. If the migrants were to settle down, they could vote and exercise political power. If they have no permanent residence, they cannot organize and threaten the ruling business elites. Yet anybody who opposes the designs of big business is automatically labeled a labor agitator and placed on the blacklist, so that he is prevented from working anywhere. The police can even murder migrant workers, for these laborers have no name and no property, and thus no power.

The family loses one more member when Connie Rivers abandons his pregnant wife. He leaves out of selfishness; he believes that he would have been better off staying in Oklahoma and that he can make a better life for himself away from the Joads. What he does out of self-interest is tantamount to treason for the Joads. Connie reveals himself to be arrogant in his belief that he can attain a middle-class lifestyle. Ma Joad, in contrast, remains the center of authority, generous and just. She gives away some food to starving children even when her family must budget its own food carefully, and even defends Connie, claiming that it is useless to criticize him for leaving.

Connie's selfish behavior is reflected in Uncle John's similar actions. Uncle John has also remained somewhat aloof from the family, keeping five dollars for himself in order to get drunk. However, even when he wishes to behave selfishly, he still makes a sacrifice for the good of the Joads, giving up more than half of his money. Unlike Connie's actions, his behavior is spurred by a heavy sense of guilt rather than a lack of concern for the others.

Nonetheless, there are indications of hope for the Joad family. The government camps are safe terrain for them, since they cannot be bothered or intimidated by police officers and can expect some comforts.

The sudden outbreak of violence is not really an unexpected event, considering the previous accounts of the California deputies' cruelty and Tom's warning that he is still capable of committing violent acts. Yet the fight is not as dramatic as one might predict: Tom does little more than trip the deputy, while Casy knocks the man unconscious. It is the deputy who causes the real havoc, inadvertently shooting an innocent woman. Still, the outcome of the event is significant for Jim Casy. He takes Tom's place as the scapegoat for the crime, sacrificing himself to save Tom. His role in the novel as a spiritual martyr is fulfilled.

Chapter Twenty-One: The hostility that the migrant workers have faced has changed them. They are now united as targets of hostility, and this unity makes the little Hooverville towns more capable of defending themselves. The larger tensions, however, have not disappeared: there was panic when the migrants multiplied on the highways. The California residents fear them, thinking them dirty, ignorant degenerates and sexual maniacs. Because the number of migrant workers has caused the wages to go down, the owners invent a new economic method: the great owners buy canneries, where they keep the price of fruit down to force smaller farmers out. Yet the owners do not know that the line between hunger and anger is a thin one.

Analysis:

This chapter returns to previously-articulated themes, explaining some of the tactics that the great owners use in order to make profits at the expense of working class farmers. Steinbeck also makes it clear that the result of such tactics will be a working class uprising, the product of perpetual poverty and oppression.

The Grapes of Wrath Chapters 22-26 Summary and Analysis

Chapter Twenty-Two: The Joads reach the government camp, where they are surprised to find that there are toilets and showers and running water. The watchman at the camp explains some of the other appealing features: there is a central committee elected by the camp residents that keeps order and makes rules, and the camp even holds dance nights. The next morning, two camp residents (Timothy and Wilkie Wallace) give Tom breakfast and tell him about a chance for work. When the men reach the fields where they are to work, Mr. Thomas, the contractor, tells them that he is reducing wages from thirty to twenty-five cents per hour. It is not his choice, but a decision dictated by the Farmers' Association, which is owned by the Bank of the West. Mr. Thomas also shows them a newspaper, which has a story about a band of citizens who burned a squatters' camp, infuriated by presumed communist agitation; he warns Tom and the other laborers about the dance at the government camp on Saturday night. According to Mr. Thomas, there will be a fight staged at the camp so that the deputies can go in. The Farmers' Association dislikes the government camps because the people in the camps become used to being treated humanely and are thus harder to handle. Tom and the Wallaces vow to make sure that there won't be a fight.

While the men work, Wilkie tells Tom that the complaints about agitators are false. According to the rich owners, any person who wants thirty cents an hour instead of twenty-five is a red. Back at the camp, Ruthie and Winfield are exploring the premises, and are fascinated by the toilets; however, they are frightened by the flushing sound. Ma Joad makes the rest of the family clean themselves up before the Ladies Committee comes to visit her. Jim Rawley, the camp manager, also introduces himself to the Joads and tells them about some of the additional features of the camp. Rose of Sharon goes to take a bath, and learns that a nurse visits the camp every week and can help her deliver the baby when the time comes. Ma remarks that she no longer feels ashamed, as she did when the Joads were constantly being harassed by the police.

Yet there are still sources of contention in the camp. Lisbeth Sandry, a religious zealot, speaks with Rose of Sharon about the alleged sin that goes on during the dances, and complains about people putting on stage plays, which she calls "sin and delusion and devil stuff." The woman even blames playacting for a mother dropping her child. Rose of Sharon becomes frightened upon hearing this, fearing that she will drop her own child. In addition, Jessie Bullitt, the head of the Ladies Committee, gives Ma Joad a tour of the camp and explains some of the problems. Jessie bickers with Ella Summers, the previous committee head.

Elsewhere, Pa comforts Uncle John, who still wants to leave and remains convinced that he will bring the family punishment. Ma Joad confronts Lisbeth Sandry for frightening Rose and for preaching that every action is sinful. Despite some of the positive developments, Ma becomes depressed about all of her losses -- Granma and Grampa, Noah and Connie -- since she now has leisure time to think about such things.

Analysis:

The government camp proves a sharp interruption to the consistent maladies and hardships that have plagued the Joad family throughout the novel. At this site, the people are polite and well-mannered toward the Joads. Ma Joad is even shocked to hear Jim Rawley call her "Mrs." The few problems in Weedpatch, such as the theft of toilet paper, are handled in a fair and organized manner. The camp represents a communal society in which everyone has an equal share and an equal voice. While not a perfect place, as shown by the unwelcome proselytizing of Lisbeth Sandry, the government camp nevertheless is a comfortable community where the Joads can live respectably.

The degree of comfort that Weedpatch affords is reflected in the return to a normal rhythm that occurs among the Joads. Ruthie and Winfield can play like small children once again. Uncle John settles into a fairly manageable routine of depression. The impressionable Rose of Sharon begins to fret about her child; without Connie, she no longer dreams of a middle-class life, but instead focuses on the immediate fate of her soon-to-be-born child. Ma Joad even realizes how great an interruption the journey to California was. For the first time, she can comprehend the losses that the family has suffered and mourn the two deaths and two desertions. Before reaching the camp, her only concern was necessarily her own survival; the most important luxury that Ma Joad discovers at the camp is introspection.

The degree of poverty to which the Joads and other migrant workers have been subjected is further underscored by the amazement that the characters show when they see the simple amenities in the camp. Ruthie and Winfield have never used toilets before, while Jessie Bullitt tells Ma Joad that some camp residents have trouble utilizing some of the camp's appliances.

Once again, the banking elite causes needless hardship for the migrant workers. The Farmers' Association that the banks control dictates that wages be reduced. It becomes clear that the Farmers' Association is responsible for most of the hardship and oppression. This organization controls the state deputies who intimidate the migrant farmers. The Farmers' Association is opposed to treating the migrant workers fairly, for if the workers expect to be treated well they will demand better work and better living conditions. The workers' enemies even plan underhanded tactics to subvert the government camps, for when the workers are secure in government camps they are actually more difficult to control. This chapter explicitly lays out the plan formed by the authorities: to sabotage the government camp, they will instigate a fight that will allow the deputies to enter and disrupt Weedpatch.

Chapter Twenty-Three: The migrant workers look for amusement wherever they can find it, whether in jokes or entertaining stories. They tell stories of heroism in taming the land and dealing with the Indians, or relate the tale of a rich man who pretended to be poor and fell in love with a rich woman who, oddly enough, was also pretending to be poor. The workers find pleasure in playing the harmonica or a more precious guitar or fiddle, or in getting drunk.

Analysis:

This chapter portrays some of the simple details of the life of a migrant worker. These workers look for amusement and diversion, for they require a respite from their hardships. Some of these amusements are not exactly innocent: drunkenness is common because it softens loneliness and pain. It essentially serves as a form of temporary suicide, dulling a man into a drunken stupor and then finally causing him to sleep. Steinbeck even writes that "death was a friend, and sleep was death's brother." While not applicable to Uncle John alone, this description of drunkenness does seem to fit with the character's depression and does give some explanation for his behavior in previous chapters.

Chapter Twenty-Four: The rumors that the police are going to break up the dance reach the camp. According to Ezra Huston, the chairman of the Central Committee, this is a frequent tactic that the police use. Huston tells Willie Eaton, the head of the Entertainment Committee, that if he must hit a deputy, he should hit the deputy in a way that doesn't draw blood. The camp members say that the Californians hate them because the migrants might draw relief without paying income taxes, but the migrants themselves quickly refute this idea, claiming that they pay sales a tax and a tobacco tax.

At the dance, Willie Eaton approaches Tom and tells him where to watch for intruders. Tom in fact locates the intruders at the dance, but the intruders begin a fight; the police enter the camp immediately. Huston confronts the police about the intruders, asking who paid them, yet the officers only admit that they have to make money somehow. Once the problem is defused, the dance goes on without any further altercations.

Analysis:

This chapter continues to illustrate how society within Weedpatch functions, showing how information goes from the elected leaders to the camp residents and how the residents maintain order. The interaction between the residents is fair and systematic; the hierarchy that has emerged among the various heads of committees and the residents with fewer responsibilities is one based on mutual respect. The committee leaders do not issue orders; at most, they offer advice and counsel to the less influential residents.

The orderly workings of Weedpatch society are reflected in how the residents react to the intruders during the dance. There is no outbreak of violence, as Steinbeck had earlier foreshadowed. Instead, the committee members deal with the situation calmly, defusing the uproar and refusing to allow the deputies and the intruders at the dance to incite a violent riot.

The rationale that the intruders give for their behavior is one that Steinbeck has frequently rejected as a justification for action. These police officials claim that they accepted the bribes given to start the riot simply in order to support themselves. This motive of self-interest has frequently been rejected by Steinbeck as untenable, whether used by a tractor driver or a small business owner. Individualistic concerns are characterized as selfish and detrimental to the public good, in clear contrast to selfless collective behavior. The intruders are the most extreme example of this selfish attitude.

Chapter Twenty-Five: Spring is beautiful in California, for the cultivation of the trees in the orchards is the responsibility of men of understanding, who experiment with the seeds and crops to make them resistant to insects and disease. Yet the fruits become rotten and soft. The rotten grapes are still used for wine, even if contaminated with mildew and formic acid. The rationale is that such wine is good enough to be a drink for the poor. The decay of the fruit spreads over the state. It becomes evident that the men who have created the new fruits cannot create a system whereby the fruits may be eaten. As Steinbeck's narrator argues, there is a crime here that goes beyond denunciation, a sorrow that weeping cannot symbolize. Children must die from pellagra because the orange business cannot be made less profitable.

Analysis:

In this chapter, Steinbeck extends his metaphor of ripening and decay among the elite business class. The wealthy owners have lavished great expense to ensure that the fruits grown on their farms are ripe and healthy, impervious to disease -- yet such tactics are the source of the eventual rot. By accumulating too much and forcing the prices of the fruit too high -- while other people have too little -- the owners ensure that nobody will be able to buy the fruit. They have engineered their own demise, yet there are more important victims in this tragedy. Children die from disease because their parents cannot afford the fruit. The young are the most direct casualties of the profit margin.

Chapter Twenty-Six: One evening, Ma Joad watches Winfield as he sleeps; he is writhing and he seems discolored. In the month that the Joads have been in Weedpatch, Tom has had only five days of work, and the rest of the men have had none. Ma worries because Rose of Sharon is close to delivering her baby. Despite these troubles, Ma reprimands the rest of the Joads for becoming discouraged. She tells them that in such circumstances they don't have the right, yet Pa fears that they will have to leave Weedpatch. When Tom mentions work in Marysville, Ma decides that they will go there, for despite the pleasant accommodations at Weedpatch the Joads have no substantial opportunities to make money.

Thus, the Joads plan to go north, where the cotton will soon be ready for harvest. Aware of Ma Joad's forceful role within the family, Pa remarks that women seem to be in control and that it may be time to get out a stick. Ma hears this, and tells him that she is doing her job as wife, but that he certainly isn't doing his job as husband. The younger family members also reflect on their relationships: Rose of Sharon complains that if Connie hadn't left the Joads would have had a house by now. Al parts ways with a blonde girl that he has been seeing; she rejects his promises that they will eventually get married. (He promises her that he'll return soon, but the girl does not believe him.) Pa remarks that he only notices that he stinks now that he takes regular baths. Before the Joads leave, Willie remarks that the deputies don't bother the residents of Weedpatch because the residents are united, and a union may be the solution to the laborers' troubles.

The car starts to break down as the Joads leave, since Al has let the battery run down, but he fixes the problem and the Joads continue on their way. Yet Al remains irritable. He says that he's going out on his own soon to start a family. On the road, the car gets a flat tire. While Tom fixes the tire, a businessman stops in his car and offers the family a job picking peaches forty miles north. The Joads reach the ranch at Pixley where they are to pick peaches for five cents a box; even the women and children can do the job. Ruthie and Winfield worry about settling down in the area and going to school in California, since they assume that everyone will regard them negatively and call them Okies.

At the nearby grocery store, which is owned by Hooper Ranch, Ma finds that the prices are much higher than they would be at the store in town. The sales clerk lends Ma ten cents for sugar. She tells him that only poor people are willing to help out. That night, Tom goes for a walk, but a deputy tells him to walk back to the cabin at the ranch. The deputy claims that if Tom is alone, the reds will get to him. While continuing on his walk, Tom finds Casy, who has been released from jail and is now with a group of men who are on strike. Casy claims that people who strive for justice always face opposition, citing Lincoln and Washington, as well as the martyrs of the French Revolution. Casy, Tom, and the rest of the strikers are confronted by the police. A short, heavy man with a white pick handle swings it at Casy, hitting him in the head. Tom fights with the man, and eventually wrenches the club from him and strikes him with it, killing him.

Tom immediately flees the scene, crawling through a stream to get back to the family's cabin. He cannot sleep that night, and in the morning tells Ma that he must hide. He tells her that he was spotted, and warns his family that they are breaking the strike: they are getting five cents a box only because of this and may get only half that amount once the strike is over. When Tom tells Ma that he is going to leave that night, she tells him that they aren't a family anymore. In her view, Al cares about nothing more than girls, Uncle John is only dragging along, Pa has lost his place as the head of the family, and the children are becoming unruly. Rose of Sharon then screams at Tom for murdering the man, since she thinks that his sin will doom her baby. In yet another blow to the Joads, after a day of work, Winfield becomes extremely sick from eating peaches. Uncle John tells Tom that when the police catch him, there will be a lynching. Tom insists that he must leave, but Ma insists that they leave as a family. The Joads make sure to hide Tom as they leave, taking the back roads to avoid detection by the police.

Analysis:

The comfortable situation that the Joads find in Weedpatch must inevitably come to an end, as the Joads realize that they cannot find work in that area. The Joads must then settle for accommodations at the Hooper Ranch, where have neither the amenities of the government camp nor the sense of a strong community. The departure from the unified society of the government camp is reflected in the breakdown of the Joad family. Even Ma Joad realizes that the family is falling apart, despite her best efforts to keep everybody together. Al has little concern for anybody else, and indicates that he is ready to leave. Pa Joad has lost his status as head of the household; he cedes complete control to Ma, the only one strong enough to keep the family in one piece. Pa Joad even makes a significant comment about gender roles, lamenting the fact that he no longer runs the family, though Ma makes it clear that the roles have changed only because he no longer fulfills his duties as husband and father. Since Ma is the only Joad who fulfills her obligations to the rest of the family -- serving as both caretaker and moral center -- she gains the right to make decisions for the rest of the family. This is the major loss that Pa suffers; he no longer has the right to decide the family's fate, and must accept that he has become his wife's subordinate.

Yet not even Ma Joad is strong enough to prevent the gradual disintegration of the Joad household. Al appears ready to abandon the Joads next; he is more concerned with finding a girl and a steady job working on cars than with helping his family support itself. In his dreams of successful, steady employment he resembles the callous Connie. Rose of Sharon in turn descends into a paranoid religious hysteria. She fears for the safety of her child and holds delusions that the murders her brother has committed will permanently scar the child with sin. It is possible to trace her ideas to the earlier influence of Lisbeth Sandry, the religious zealot who warned Rose of Sharon against sin. Even the two very young children begin to suffer noticeably: Winfield becomes sick from deprivation.

The conditions at the Hooper Ranch are worse than those at the government camp, but still not as bad as they could be. The Joads have a roof over their heads and are paid sufficient wages. However, the store owned by the ranch artificially raises the prices of items -- for it is only at the nearby store that the workers can buy groceries -- and the wages are high initially only because of a strike. Ma Joad makes the significant observation at the grocery store that only the poor will help other impoverished people; the clerk at the grocery store will assist her, but the owners of the grocery store will exploit the workers by setting inflated prices.

The strike is the catalyst of another tragedy for the Joad family. Soon after Tom finds the striking workers, he is reunited with Jim Casy, who has been released from jail and has found a new purpose as a labor activist. His lost religious zeal has been transformed into working-class activism, charged by his experiences in jail and his travels within California. Casy is a crusader for the cause of the workers; the indecision over his role as a preacher earlier in the novel has been replaced by a fiery conviction concerning the justice of laborers' rights. There are strong political overtones to the final scenes with Casy, who compares the cause of labor to the missions of Lincoln, Washington, and the patriots of the French Revolution. Steinbeck makes it clear that the labor activists are facing certain doom, but that they will be vindicated eventually. Casy, who sacrificed his freedom for Tom earlier in the novel, makes a final sacrifice in this chapter, the victim of a brutal murder at the hands of the police. Casy has now been a martyr for both the Joad family and the entire class that the Joads represent.

The effect of this martyrdom is that Tom must now leave Hooper ranch to escape capture by the police. Although he wishes to go alone, Ma Joad once again binds the Joad family together. She chooses to risk the safety of the entire family to preserve whatever unity the family has left.

The Grapes of Wrath Chapters 27-30 Summary and Analysis

Chapter Twenty-Seven: Those who want to pick cotton must first purchase a bag before they can make money. The men who weigh the cotton fix the scales to cheat the workers. On account of the growing industrialization of agriculture, the introduction of a cotton-picking machine seems inevitable.

Analysis:

Steinbeck here exposes several additional sources of fraud in the farming system. The owners who hire the cotton pickers seem intent on making sure that the pickers receive lower compensation than they deserve, and place these laborers in initial debt by making them pay for cotton bags beforehand. The system is made to maximize profit, no matter the cost to the worker. The only solution that the workers have is confrontation: they must stand up to the men who weigh the cotton and actively ensure that they are paid fairly.

Chapter Twenty-Eight: The Joads are now staying in a boxcar that stands beside a stream, a small home that proves better than any other residence, except for the quarters at the government camp. They are now picking cotton. Winfield tells Ma that Ruthie told got into an argument with some other kids and told them that her brother Tom was on the run for committing murder. Ruthie returns to Ma, crying that the kids stole her Cracker Jack -- the reason that she threatened them by telling about Tom -- but Ma tells Ruthie that it was her own fault for showing off her candy to others.

That night, in the pitch black, Ma Joad goes out into the woods and finds Tom, who has been hiding. She crawls close to him and wants to touch him to remember what he looks like. She also wants to give him seven dollars to take the bus and get away. He tells her that he has been thinking about Casy; Tom remembers that Casy went out into the woods searching for his soul, but only found that he had no individual soul, only part of a larger one. Tom has been wondering why people can't work together for their living, and vows to do what Casy had done. He leaves, but promises to return to the family when everything has blown over.

As she leaves Tom, Ma Joad does not cry. However, rain begins to fall. Upon her return to the boxcar, Ma meets Mr. and Mrs. Wainwright, who have come to talk to the Joads about their daughter, Aggie, who has been spending time with Al. The Wainwrights are worried that the two families will part and that they will then find out that Aggie is pregnant. Pa laments leaving Oklahoma, while Ma says that women can deal with change better than men, because women have their lives in their arms and men have theirs in their heads. For women, change is more acceptable because it seems inevitable.

Al and Aggie return to the boxcar, where they announce that they are getting married. They go out before dawn to pick cotton before everyone else and Rose of Sharon vows to go with them, even though she can barely move. When the Joads get to the place where the cotton is being picked, they discover that other families are already present. While the cotton picking continues, rain begins to fall, causing Rose of Sharon to fall ill. Everybody assumes that the young woman is about to deliver her child, but they discover instead that she is suffering from a chill. They take her back to the boxcar and start a fire to get her warm.

Analysis:

The Joads settle once again into a temporary home -- this time a boxcar -- but find their routine disrupted one more time when Ruthie reveals the secret about Tom. Significantly, the cause of Ruthie's fight with the other children is arrogance; by eating her candy out in the open, she offends the other children, who are starving. Tom's decision to leave the family is a bittersweet event, but entirely inevitable. By remaining with the family, he would place them in danger and make himself a burden, since he cannot contribute to their labor.

When Tom does decide to leave the Joad family, he does so with a new purpose that is a combination of political and spiritual belief. Tom accepts Casy's teaching that there is no individual soul, only a collective soul of which each person possesses only a part. With these new convictions in mind, he vows to continue Casy's struggle for better treatment of the workers. This is a turning point for Tom, who previously consigned himself to individualistic action for himself and his family but now wishes to work for the common good.

It is Ma Joad who bids farewell to Tom, proving herself once again to be the center of the Joad family. She also changes her own ideals in this chapter; she advises Tom to go alone, abandoning her earlier attempts to keep the family together at almost any cost. She has realized that family unity is insignificant without the greater social unity for which Tom will strive. Furthermore, even though Tom is the character for whom Ma has shown the most affection, she finds that she cannot weep over his departure. Rather, at the moment when she realizes she cannot cry, the rainfall begins -- a natural phenomenon that reflects her emotional state.

Steinbeck suggests in this chapter that women such as Ma Joad are better equipped to handle change and pain than men are. During the course of the novel, the men have often railed against their fates: Uncle John and Connie desert the family, while Grampa dies shortly after he is forced to leave Oklahoma. Ma Joad, in contrast, has accepted the changes she has faced. She explains that women can accept change because, for them, it is inevitable. They do not have the illusion that they control their own destinies, in evident contrast to men. Thus, they are less shaken when they are presented with hardship.

The immaturity that Al Joad has displayed throughout the novel takes a more dangerous edge in this chapter. Mr. and Mrs. Wainwright confront the Joads with the possibility that Al could get their daughter pregnant, leaving her with the burden of a child and little (or no) support. Even the announcement of Al and Aggie's engagement is not especially joyful news, since Steinbeck contrasts the engagement with the pregnancy of Rose of Sharon, who is ready to deliver her child without her husband or any other strong male influence to sustain her.

Chapter Twenty-Nine: The migrant families wonder how long the rain will last. The rain damages cars and penetrates tents. During the rain storms some people go to relief offices, but there are rules: one is required to live in California for a year before one can collect relief. The greatest terror has arrived -- no work available for a stretch of three months. Hungry men crowd the alleys to beg for bread; a number of people die. Anger festers, causing sheriffs to swear in new deputies. There will be no work and no food.

Analysis:

The migrant workers must face yet another hardship, this one perhaps the worst of all. With the coming of the rains comes the end of the harvest season. The migrant workers face starvation, yet cannot receive any government relief. For Steinbeck, the treatment of these workers is not merely inhumane; such treatment is below even the treatment of livestock. Steinbeck's narrative makes the point that no farm owner would leave his horse to starve when it was not used. However, the farm owners are allowing starvation to afflict the migrant labor force.

Chapter Thirty: After three days of rain, the Wainwrights decide that they must continue on their way. They fear that the creek will flood; however, Rose of Sharon goes into labor and the Joads, consequently, cannot leave. Even though Pa Joad and the rest of the men at the camp build up the embankment to prevent flooding, the water breaks through. Pa, Al, and Uncle John then rush toward the car, but it cannot start. They reach the boxcar and find that Rose of Sharon has delivered a stillborn baby.

The Joads realize that their car will eventually flood; Mr. Wainwright blames Pa Joad for asking the Wainwrights to stay and help, but Mrs. Wainwright offers the Joads her sympathy. She tells Ma Joad that it once was the case that family came first. Yet now the migrants have greater concerns. Uncle John places Rose of Sharon's dead baby in an apple box and floats it down the flooded stream as the other Joads build a platform on the top of the car. As the flood waters rise, the family remains on the platform. However, the family must eventually re-locate and finds a barn for refuge until the rain stops. In the corner of this barn are a starving man and a boy. Ma makes everybody leave the barn, while Rose of Sharon gives the severely weakend man her breast milk.

Analysis:

The Joads are caught in a dilemma in this chapter. They face the possibility that the nearby creek will flood, but cannot leave because Rose of Sharon goes into labor. The one solution to their dire situation depends on community action: the rest of the families must pitch in to build up the embankment, which will stop the flooding.

Nonetheless, most of the families selfishly suggest departure, reasoning that they have no obligation to help Rose of Sharon. Because they are left without assistance, the Joads are forced to take shelter on top of their car when the stream floods.

Mrs. Wainwright's comment that there are now greater concerns than family highlights Steinbeck's collectivist stance in *The Grapes of Wrath.* It has taken overwhelming poverty and hardship for groups such as the Joads to realize that the small, isolated families must come together for united action.

In establishing this chapter's tone of urgency, the birth of Rose of Sharon's child carries significant symbolic meanings. For Rose of Sharon, the child has represented the possibilities for the future, yet the baby is stillborn. The event has clear parallels to the Joads' journey to California: they have faced incredible hardship and pain striving for a better future, yet their sacrifices have led to nothing. The fate of the baby is even a perverse reversal of religious imagery. Uncle John places the dead child in a box and sends it down the river, an obvious and darkly ironic allusion to Moses. Instead of a living savior, this vessel offers a dead omen.

Yet the final scene in *The Grapes of Wrath* is one meant to instill a modicum of hope. The debilitated Rose of Sharon breastfeeds the starving man in the barn to sustain him. She gives what was meant for her baby to a complete stranger, an example of selfless sacrifice for the sake of community instead of adherence to individual well-being. It took a deep personal loss, the delivery of a stillborn child, to enable Rose of Sharon to aid the man. She nonetheless cares for the anonymous man with a measure of the same love she might have shown her own child, eschewing her selfish concerns for a communal good.

The Grapes of Wrath The Grapes of Wrath and Censorship

For the most part, *The Grapes of Wrath* was met with praise when it appeared; in 1939 it was the best-selling American novel, according to *The New York Times*. It sold more than 430,000 copies in February 1940, and it went on to become one of the most widely discussed books of the 20th century. Despite this tremendous success, Steinbeck's novel also ruffled feathers and caused controversy. Yet Steinbeck embraced this controversy and had even prepared for such backlash as he was composing the novel. As he famously declared before *The Grapes of Wrath* was published, "I want to put a tag of shame on the greedy bastards who are responsible for this. I've done my damnedest to rip a reader's nerves to rags."

The book was indeed banned in some schools, particularly in places where the Associated Farmers had a strong presence. In Kern County, California, the Associated Farmers began burning the book and had it banned from the local library. The librarian, Gretchen Knief, worked to overturn the ban; nonetheless, local prohibitions on the book held for 1 1/2 years. After this ban was eventually overturned, interest in censorship issues led to the creation of the Library Bill of Rights. Steinbeck's novel has continued to face some censorship, but for the most part the book is widely available and strongly celebrated.

The Grapes of Wrath The Grapes of Wrath (Film Version, 1940)

The Grapes of Wrath was transformed into a film in 1940. Directed by John Ford, the movie version of Steinbeck's famous novel also ranks as Ford's most famous black-and-white creation. The film has been praised for its honest and realistic portrayal of the socio-economic impact of the Great Depression, and for its depiction of the great drought of the mid 1930s. Consistently true to its source, the film closely follows the novel's plot and development. One of the most famous left-leaning films to appear just before America entered World War II, *The Grapes of Wrath* was nominated for 7 Academy Awards and took home two of these. Jane Darwell won Best Supporting Actress for her role as the archetypal mother figure Ma Joad, and John Ford won the award for Best Director. The film is still remembered as a great work of art.

The Grapes of Wrath Revisiting The Grapes of Wrath

In 2013, the National Steinbeck Center commissioned three artists and researchers to retrace the route of the characters in *The Grapes of Wrath*. The researchers reported back that they had experienced many of the same weather conditions that Steinbeck wrote about in his novel, and that they also had witnessed many people suffering through the kind of rural poverty that afflicted Steinbeck's characters. When *The Grapes of Wrath* was first published, critics believed that it would be limited by its distinctive 1930s setting. However, the reports of these researchers have shown that Steinbeck's work is timeless and not bound by the narrative of the Dust Bowl: the landscapes and the hardships it depicts have not disappeared from 20th-century America.

The Grapes of Wrath Links

National Steinbeck Center

http://www.steinbeck.org/

The website of a national institution devoted to Steinbeck. Includes information about the museum as well as about Steinbeck's life and work.

The Grapes of Wrath (1940)

http://www.imdb.com/title/tt0032551/

Information on the cinematic version of *The Grapes of Wrath*, which was produced in 1940.

The Grapes of Wrath (1940)

http://www.filmsite.org/grap.html

Film review of *The Grapes of Wrath* (1940)

Teacher Resources

http://www.steinbeckinstitute.org/teacher.html

Lesson plans and other teacher resources, produced by the National Steinbeck Center.

Grapes of Wrath Is 75, But Its Depictions of Poverty Are Timeless

http://www.npr.org/2014/04/14/301833421/grapes-of-wrath-is-75-but-its-depictions-of-poverty-are-timeless

A recent article on the themes of *The Grapes of Wrath* and how they relate to the world today.

The Grapes of Wrath Essay Questions

1. **How does the dialogue in *The Grapes of Wrath* work to illustrate the setting of the novel?**

   Steinbeck uses broken language and colloquialisms in the dialogue between his characters, and (as written out) the conversations are littered with misspellings. The dialogue can be difficult to read at times, but it serves to illustrate the mood and atmosphere of the characters and their lives: although the Joads and their companions are not prosperous or highly educated, they talk in a way that they can understand easily among themselves. Even though it takes patience to decipher, Steinbeck's dialogue is key to an accurate portrayal of how migrant workers spoke and interacted with one another.

2. **Provide and explain instances from the novel when the characters realize the enormity of the systemic injustices perpetrated against them.**

   There are many examples of moral awareness in the novel, and such awareness occurs in monologues, narratives, and conversations between characters. All of these are important to answering this question, and it would be best to include a variety of examples in order to compare and contrast different episodes. For example, it would be effective to include a passage that does not include major characters (such as the scene in which an unnamed tenant argues with an unnamed tractor driver), and contrast such a scene with Muley's monologue about profit margin. In this exchange, Muley addresses two very important characters, Casy and Joad, shortly after seeing them for the first time.

3. **How does alternating between generic and specific scenes further the plot and the emotional effect of the novel?**

   The answer to this question should explain how the novel alternates between narrative descriptions of generic scenes, where no characters are known or named, and lengthier chapters that deal with the characters that have been formally introduced to the reader. Because the generic scenes come first, they provide backdrops for the events that are about to face the major characters, such as Tom Joad, Ma, or Jim Casy. In Steinbeck's novel, the use of juxtaposition highlights the universality of certain experiences and allows the reader to see the far-reaching effects of what the Joad family is experiencing.

4. **Describe the relationship between the people and their land in *The Grapes of Wrath*.**

   The answer to this question should delve into the many passages in the beginning of the novel that discuss the primal connection between man and the land. When the tractor destroys homes and removes people from the land, this machine is excising portions of human livelihood and memory. Additionally, when a person is forced to leave and will no longer know whether there is a willow tree out front, then that individual has been forced to leave behind an essential part of his or her being. The process of moving is a process of upheaval, both physically and emotionally, since the people are forced to leave behind the things that they hold dear.

5. **How do the Joads handle the uncertainty of their future in California?**

   While the Joads, and many other families, have been promised a land of plentiful produce and good employment in California, these families are still unsure about whether the handbills are telling the truth. Each of the Joads handles the uncertainty differently: Ma focuses only on each day and on taking care of her family from moment to moment, Tom tries to think of nothing in the future (just as he did in prison), and Pa thinks fondly of the produce that he will be able to pick and eat in California. Even though the Joads all discuss the future in different ways, a basic anxiety and uncertainty lies beneath all of their conversations about the future.

6. **How do the Joads handle the difficulties of the journey to California? Exactly what obstances must the family face?**

   The Joads must take care of their limited money and must make due with small living spaces as they travel to California. They have 12 people and many possessions packed on the back of an old jalopy, and the physical elements make the journey unpleasant: the family is exposed to weather conditions constantly. Emotionally, they face obstacles as well: they lose Granma and Grampa en route, and Ma also becomes very sick. In addition, they meet a handful of people who tell them that California doesn't actually offer all that the handbills claim. Despite the doubts introduced by other people and despite their own personal doubts, the Joads continue on. They remain optimistic and believe that, even if other families have faced difficulties, they will be able to find work, save money, and create a better life.

7. **Why did the number of handbills printed exceed the amount of work available? How does this relate to capitalism and organized labor?**

   When answering this question, keep in mind that almost every family traveling west has seen the orange handbill which declares that hundreds of field workers are needed. The Joads refuse to believe that an excess number of handbills would have been printed because printing handbills costs money, but other travelers explain that all this is part of a larger strategy. If there is an excess number of workers, the owners of the land have leverage and can drive pay rates down because men are desperate for work and need to feed their families. Without the organized labor that could stand up to the capitalist owners, the laborers are at the mercy of their bosses. The struggle between capitalism and organized labor is a prominent theme in *The Grapes of Wrath*, and this theme should be expanded upon in the answer to this essay question.

8. **Why do the wealthy landowners feel threatened by the government camp, and what do they do about it?**

   The wealthy landowners and businessmen have built a formidable opposition to the demands of the laborers, who seek essential human rights and basic lifestyle improvements. In Steinbeck's narrative, the business interests have accumulated an enormous surplus of workers, so that now these interests can easily control labor wages. But because the laborers are staying in a government camp where they are able to elect their own leaders, have their voices heard, and live in a dignified manner, the landowners are concerned that the laborers' frustration with the economic system will grow into a rebellion. In order to stop this, the landowners have planned for a fight to happen at a labor camp dance, which will enable police officers to enter and end the tranquil and confident life of the camp.

9. **What is the meaning of the title, *The Grapes of Wrath*? Where does it appear in the novel?**

   The answer to this question should explain that the title of the book appears at the very end of the novel, in a long narrative quote. The answer should also explain the phrase's origins in the Book of Revelation and the Battle Hymn of the Republic. In addition, an effective essay on this topic should acknowledge that there have been different interpretations of the title; still, try to offer an explanation that points to the broader themes of the novel, such as oppression, greed, suffering, and justice.

10. **How does labor organizing bring the hope of better labor conditions?**

    For the migrants depicted in *The Grapes of Wrath*, wages have been driven down by a high supply of laborers and a low demand for work. Internal competition for jobs has driven these wages even lower. Laborers who form organizations are able to communicate with one another and to call attention to wages that are lower than they are willing to accept -- wages that they cannot survive on. By gathering together, laborers have greater leverage against powerful landowners.

The Grapes of Wrath Quizzes

1. **What weather event does the first chapter describe?**
   A. The San Francisco Earthquake
   B. The Tri-State Tornado of 1925
   C. The Galveston Hurricane of 1900
   D. The Dust Bowl

2. **Where has Tom Joad been released from just before he hitches a ride on a truck?**
   A. Jail
   B. Previous job
   C. Mental facility
   D. Hospital

3. **Why did Tom Joad serve time in jail?**
   A. Arson
   B. Robbery
   C. Homicide
   D. Rape

4. **What animal does Tom Joad pick up in the road?**
   A. Rabbit
   B. Dog
   C. Turtle
   D. Cat

5. **Whom does Tom Joad meet on his way home from jail?**
   A. Jim Casy
   B. Al Joad
   C. Ma Joad
   D. Pa Joad

6. **What occupation did Jim Casy previously have?**
   A. Salesman
   B. Preacher
   C. Contractor
   D. Farmer

7. **How did Jim Casy take advantage of his position of authority?**
   A. Financial embezzlement
   B. Labor manipulation
   C. Alcohol bootlegging
   D. Sexual relationships

8. **Which of the following is NOT true of the murder Tom Joad committed?**
   A. He hit his opponent with a shovel.
   B. He was in a fight.
   C. He was attacking a family member.
   D. He was stabbed.

9. **How did the Joads acquire their house?**
   A. They bought it from a friend.
   B. They bought it from a land agent.
   C. They built it.
   D. They stole it.

10. **Why is Tom Joad out of jail?**
   A. He escaped.
   B. He has been released on parole.
   C. He was found innocent.
   D. His sentence is finished.

11. **What pushed the Oklahoma tenants off of their land?**
   A. Organized crime
   B. Industrialized farming
   C. Migrant workers
   D. Health precautions

12. **In the novel, what inanimate object is frequently referred to as a "monster?"**
   A. Hospital
   B. Bank
   C. Farm
   D. Church

13. **Where do the landowners suggest that the Oklahoma tenants go?**
   A. Oregon
   B. California
   C. Boston
   D. New York

14. **Whom would Muley NOT describe as one of "Them sons-a-bitches?"**
   A. Industrial agriculture
   B. Tom Joad
   C. "Owner men"
   D. Banks

15. **What does Tom Joad see when he first arrives at his home?**
A. His whole family, eagerly awaiting his arrival
B. The foundation of his demolished house
C. The new family that has moved into his home
D. The dilapidated, collapsed shell of his house

16. **What does Tom Joad infer when he sees that the scrap parts of the Joad house remain?**
A. His family must have been evicted.
B. There are no neighbors living in the area, because nobody has taken parts off the house.
C. There must have been a fire that destroyed the house from the inside out.
D. His family must have left to go visit him in jail, and will probably reach home very soon.

17. **Where is Joad's family, according to Muley?**
A. In New York
B. At Uncle John's house
C. En route to the prison
D. In California

18. **Why are the people being kicked off the land, according to Muley?**
A. Excessively high crime rate
B. Efforts to increase profit margins
C. Corrupt police force
D. Voluntary and willing departures

19. **What does Muley frequently call himself?**
A. Damn ol' graveyard ghos'
B. Monster Man
C. The Ol' Vigilante
D. The Fighter

20. **What does Casy decide he will do after Tom Joad reunites with his family?**
A. Stay with Joad and his family, traveling wherever they travel
B. Stay on the land and begin preaching again
C. Say goodbye and move on
D. Hitch-hike to California

21. **Why is the used car industry booming?**
A. People are trying to move out to California.
B. People are hoping to sell cars for scrap metal.
C. People want to drive to different banks and talk to the employees.
D. People are buying better cars using big business profits.

22. **When Joad arrives at his Uncle's house, what does he discover?**
   A. His family is not there.
   B. His father has left his mother.
   C. His family is nearly ready to leave for California.
   D. His family has decided not to move to California.

23. **How does Joad's mother react when she sees him for the first time?**
   A. Fury that he was in jail in the first place
   B. Overwhelmingly joy
   C. Some joy, then control of her emotions
   D. Deep sadness and remorse

24. **Which adjective best describes Noah's demeanor?**
   A. Calm
   B. Quick to anger
   C. Emotional
   D. Flamboyant

25. **How does the Joad family envision California?**
   A. Dangerous and filled with possible enemies
   B. Filled with opportunities for easy fame
   C. Dry and in a drought
   D. Filled with abundant produce that can be sold

Quiz 1 Answer Key

1. **(D)** The Dust Bowl
2. **(A)** Jail
3. **(C)** Homicide
4. **(C)** Turtle
5. **(A)** Jim Casy
6. **(B)** Preacher
7. **(D)** Sexual relationships
8. **(C)** He was attacking a family member.
9. **(D)** They stole it.
10. **(B)** He has been released on parole.
11. **(B)** Industrialized farming
12. **(B)** Bank
13. **(B)** California
14. **(B)** Tom Joad
15. **(D)** The dilapidated, collapsed shell of his house
16. **(B)** There are no neighbors living in the area, because nobody has taken parts off the house.
17. **(B)** At Uncle John's house
18. **(B)** Efforts to increase profit margins
19. **(A)** Damn ol' graveyard ghos'
20. **(A)** Stay with Joad and his family, traveling wherever they travel
21. **(A)** People are trying to move out to California.
22. **(C)** His family is nearly ready to leave for California.
23. **(C)** Some joy, then control of her emotions
24. **(A)** Calm
25. **(D)** Filled with abundant produce that can be sold

The Grapes of Wrath Quizzes

1. **What is one reason why Tom Joad's younger brother, Al, admires Tom?**
   A. He escaped from jail.
   B. He respects his parents.
   C. He has slept with many women.
   D. He killed a man.

2. **What do the generic scenes, with unnamed characters, contribute to the novel?**
   A. Insight into the mind of Tom Joad
   B. Unrealistic fantasies
   C. Slapstick comedy
   D. Universality

3. **How do the Joads learn about the presumed benefits of California?**
   A. Radio Commercials
   B. Billboards
   C. Movie theater commercials
   D. Handbills

4. **What happened when the Joads, and others, tried to sell their belongings?**
   A. They decided not to sell anything.
   B. They made respectable profits.
   C. They were forced to sell for very low prices.
   D. They decided to donate rather than sell.

5. **What best describes the condition of the Joads' car before they leave?**
   A. Excellent
   B. It does not work at all.
   C. Used, but in good condition
   D. Barely working

6. **Who is chiefly responsible for the maintenance and inspection of the family car?**
   A. Al
   B. Grandpa
   C. Ma
   D. Pa

7. **What crop has been farmed in large amounts on the land?**
    A. Soybeans
    B. Wheat
    C. Corn
    D. Cotton

8. **How does the Joad family get Grandpa to go to California?**
    A. They tell him he will find gold there.
    B. They tell him about the food there.
    C. They drug him and carry him onto the truck.
    D. They tell him he will be famous and respected.

9. **What would be a violation of Tom Joad's parole?**
    A. Associating with Muley
    B. Being unemployed
    C. Living near the jail
    D. Crossing the state line

10. **What was the main route used to travel to California?**
    A. Route 66
    B. Route 90
    C. Route 44
    D. Route 83

11. **What best describes Ma's attitude regarding the move to California?**
    A. Overly excited
    B. Anxiety-ridden
    C. Angry and depressed
    D. Cautiously optimistic

12. **What word best describes Connie and Rosasharn's shared attitude?**
    A. Depressed
    B. Quick to anger
    C. Secretive
    D. Bipolar

13. **What happens to Grampa on the first night of the trip?**
    A. He has a seizure.
    B. He breaks his leg.
    C. He has a heart attack.
    D. He dies.

14. **What key issue do the Joads face after Grampa's death?**
    A. Which other people to leave people behind
    B. A doctor's visit for Ma Joad
    C. Grampa's burial fees
    D. Whether to turn around and go home

15. **How do the Joads avoid an investigation of Grampa's death?**
    A. They call a coroner.
    B. They contact a local town hall.
    C. They call the police.
    D. They leave a note with the burial.

16. **Why does Al worry about the mountains on the family's route?**
    A. He thinks that there will be too much traffic.
    B. He thinks that the car will break down.
    C. He worries about thieves.
    D. He thinks that the weather will be too cold.

17. **Who decides to join the Joad caravan?**
    A. The Smiths
    B. A few orphaned children
    C. A social worker
    D. The Wilsons

18. **When the Joads consider splitting up, who opposes this plan?**
    A. Ma
    B. Al
    C. Pa
    D. Tom

19. **Whom do the diner workers consider the best customers?**
    A. Anyone who stops
    B. Truck drivers
    C. People like the Joads
    D. Wealthy travelers

20. **What percentage of people are traveling west?**
    A. Nearly 100%
    B. 10%
    C. 20%
    D. 50%

21. **When Tom and Al go to buy a spare part, what affliction does the vendor have?**
    A. Paralyzed
    B. Missing an arm
    C. One-eyed
    D. Epilepsy

22. **What does the old man who is returning from California NOT tell the Joads?**

A. His children died there.
B. The produce industry is not making profits.
C. His wife died there.
D. The handbills make false promises.

23. **Why do the Joads consider splitting up their traveling caravan?**

A. One of the cars has a severe mechanical issue.
B. Different members of the group are frustrated with each other.
C. Part of the group is very sick
D. There is not enough money for everyone to survive.

24. **Which one of the characters pregnant?**

A. Aggie
B. Ma
C. Sairy Wilson
D. Rose of Sharon

25. **In what state does the novel open?**

A. Oklahoma
B. New York
C. Texas
D. California

Quiz 2 Answer Key

1. **(D)** He killed a man.
2. **(D)** Universality
3. **(D)** Handbills
4. **(C)** They were forced to sell for very low prices.
5. **(D)** Barely working
6. **(A)** Al
7. **(D)** Cotton
8. **(C)** They drug him and carry him onto the truck.
9. **(D)** Crossing the state line
10. **(A)** Route 66
11. **(D)** Cautiously optimistic
12. **(C)** Secretive
13. **(D)** He dies.
14. **(C)** Grampa's burial fees
15. **(D)** They leave a note with the burial.
16. **(B)** He thinks that the car will break down.
17. **(D)** The Wilsons
18. **(A)** Ma
19. **(B)** Truck drivers
20. **(A)** Nearly 100%
21. **(C)** One-eyed
22. **(B)** The produce industry is not making profits.
23. **(A)** One of the cars has a severe mechanical issue.
24. **(D)** Rose of Sharon
25. **(A)** Oklahoma

The Grapes of Wrath Quizzes

1. **What major river do the Joads cross as they approach California?**
   A. Colorado River
   B. Rio Conchos River
   C. Mississippi River
   D. Missouri River

2. **Does California appear to be prosperous when the Joads cross the border?**
   A. Yes, overwhelmingly so
   B. Somewhat
   C. Only in a few isolated places
   D. No

3. **How are the people of California described?**
   A. Mean
   B. Happy
   C. Humorous
   D. Kind

4. **Which is NOT a meaning of the word "Okie"?**
   A. A poor, dirty migrant
   B. A deeply religious person
   C. A person from Oklahoma
   D. An ignorant, uneducated person

5. **Who leaves the Joad group when the family first enters California?**
   A. Noah
   B. Al
   C. Tom
   D. Pa

6. **Where does Granma die?**
   A. In an orchard where the Joads are working in California
   B. In the Weedpatch labor camp
   C. In the truck as the Joads pass through California
   D. In Oklahoma

7. **Why do the Wilsons part with the Joads?**
   A. Sairy and Ma have a fight.
   B. Ma Joad is sick.
   C. Sairy Wilson is sick.
   D. Pa and Mr. Wilson have a fight.

8. **What do people returning east NOT tell the Joads about California?**
   A. All of the land is already owned.
   B. They will not have consistent work.
   C. Work is hard to find.
   D. There is work in the cities.

9. **What happened to people who tried to farm part of the owned California land?**
   A. They were ignored.
   B. They were allowed to stay.
   C. They were kicked off the land by the police.
   D. They were allowed to stay but they needed to pay heavy fines.

10. **How do the Joads respond to the negative descriptions of California?**
   A. They decide to turn around and return home.
   B. They decide to stay where they are and start a new life there.
   C. They keep going on their journey into the state.
   D. They proceed but are constantly tempted to turn around and return home.

11. **As described in Steinbeck's novel, what is a blacklist?**
   A. A list of owners who will not hire workers
   B. A list of farms that will not be worked
   C. A list of workers who will not be employed
   D. A list of owners who will not pay fair wages

12. **Why were handbills printed en masse?**
   A. To promote important California landmarks
   B. To ensure that just enough workers appeared
   C. To create a surplus of workers
   D. To fulfill a set of budgetary rules

13. **Why is work hard to find in California?**
   A. The workers have begun to vandalize company property.
   B. The number of workers exceeds the number of jobs.
   C. There is a drought and the food is rotten.
   D. The owners can't afford to pay the laborers.

14. **How are the characters advised to act in the presence of the police?**
   A. Aggressive
   B. "Bull simple"
   C. Submissive
   D. Excessively polite

15. **Who immediately thinks it would have been better to stay in Oklahoma?**
A. Connie
B. Tom
C. Al
D. Pa

16. **Where would be one of the best places for the Joads in California?**
A. Farther south
B. Up north
C. A Government Camp
D. A Hooverville

17. **What is NOT an amenity of the government camp?**
A. Dances
B. No police
C. Better cars
D. Hot water

18. **What does "talkin' red" mean?**
A. Discussing fresh produce
B. Appreciating the beauty of nature
C. Considering communism and organized labor
D. Bragging about crimes

19. **Why does Casy confess to a crime he didn't commit?**
A. He feels he hasn't contributed to his group yet.
B. He is drunk.
C. He committed a similar crime in the past but was never convicted.
D. He knows he'll be fed in jail.

20. **What is NOT a reason why the police burn settlements?**
A. To stop laborers from organizing
B. To intimidate those who try to protest unjust conditions
C. To keep people moving and unsettle them
D. To kill organized labor leaders

21. **What is NOT an appropriate description of the government camp?**
A. Clean
B. Communal
C. Democratic
D. Sparsely populated

22. **Who controls the wages?**
   A. Laborers
   B. Plot owners
   C. Farmers Association
   D. Police

23. **Why does Thomas warn the men about one of the camp dances?**
   A. The Farmers Association is going to cancel it.
   B. The police will forcibly prevent people from attending.
   C. The authorities have planted troublemakers to start a fight, so officers can enter.
   D. The building where the dance will be held could catch on fire.

24. **What have people "gotten used to" in the government camps?**
   A. Being constantly hungry
   B. Having steady work
   C. Being treated as humans
   D. Dirty living conditions

25. **What does the manager realize has happened when pregnant women "drop babies"?**
   A. They are sinful.
   B. They are malnourished and exhausted.
   C. The devil is inside of them.
   D. They have had abortions.

Quiz 3 Answer Key

1. **(A)** Colorado River
2. **(D)** No
3. **(A)** Mean
4. **(B)** A deeply religious person
5. **(A)** Noah
6. **(C)** In the truck as the Joads pass through California
7. **(C)** Sairy Wilson is sick.
8. **(D)** There is work in the cities.
9. **(C)** They were kicked off the land by the police.
10. **(C)** They keep going on their journey into the state.
11. **(C)** A list of workers who will not be employed
12. **(C)** To create a surplus of workers
13. **(B)** The number of workers exceeds the number of jobs.
14. **(B)** "Bull simple"
15. **(A)** Connie
16. **(C)** A Government Camp
17. **(C)** Better cars
18. **(C)** Considering communism and organized labor
19. **(A)** He feels he hasn't contributed to his group yet.
20. **(D)** To kill organized labor leaders
21. **(D)** Sparsely populated
22. **(C)** Farmers Association
23. **(C)** The authorities have planted troublemakers to start a fight, so officers can enter.
24. **(C)** Being treated as humans
25. **(B)** They are malnourished and exhausted.

The Grapes of Wrath Quizzes

1. **Why is there a credit system at the camp store?**
    A. To prevent hunger
    B. To sell relatively expensive luxury goods
    C. To bring people into debt
    D. To create reliance on the store

2. **How do the people of the West react to the arrival of the Okies?**
    A. With abiding respect
    B. With enthusiastic joy
    C. With indifference
    D. With anger and hostility

3. **Why do Rose of Sharon and the rest of the Joads become upset with Connie?**
    A. He hits Rose of Sharon.
    B. He abandons Rose of Sharon.
    C. He won't stop talking about having ice in his home.
    D. He is very critical of Pa.

4. **What happens when there is a surplus of workers competing for jobs?**
    A. More work opens up
    B. Wages are driven up
    C. Wages are driven down
    D. Wages stay stable

5. **Who makes decisions in the government camp?**
    A. The landowners
    B. The police
    C. The people, through the Central Committee
    D. The manager

6. **Why were resources devoted to protecting the dance at the government camp?**
    A. The camp officials heard that some people were upset with the musical selections.
    B. The camp store had run out of food, and the camp residents were upset.
    C. Such uses of resources were customary.
    D. Police had tried to stage a riot.

7. **Which is NOT a reason why the police tried to stage a riot at the government camp?**
   A. They were upset with the conditions at the government camp.
   B. The wanted to confiscate the residents' belongings.
   C. They wanted to break up the government camp.
   D. They couldn't enter the camp without a warrant or probable cause.

8. **Which is NOT a reason behind the discussions of unionization?**
   A. Unfair labor conditions
   B. Increasing job competition
   C. Hope of higher wages
   D. Knowledge of Marxist writings

9. **Who urges the Joads to leave the government camp despite its amenities?**
   A. Tom
   B. Pa
   C. Ma
   D. Al

10. **What kind of work are the Joads offered?**
    A. Picking peaches
    B. Laying pipe
    C. Picking cotton
    D. Building barns

11. **What is going on outside the peach farm when the Joads enter?**
    A. A strike
    B. A fire
    C. A celebration
    D. A riot

12. **How are the Joads paid for their work on the peach farm?**
    A. By each peach picked
    B. By each box they fill
    C. By the day
    D. By the hour

13. **What is unusual about the prices in the camp store at the peach farm?**
    A. They are deflated.
    B. Many of the goods are free to the laborers.
    C. They are inflated.
    D. They are perfectly fair.

14. **What happens during a strike involving Casy and Tom Joad?**
A. Casy is killed and Tom attacks an officer.
B. The men are peacefully broken up.
C. Several police officers are killed.
D. Casy and Tom escape and flee with the rest of the Joads.

15. **Why does Winfield get sick at the peach farm?**
A. He eats spoiled meat.
B. The weather is very cold at night.
C. He spends too much time in the sun.
D. He eats too many peaches.

16. **During what decade did the Dust Bowl take place?**
A. 1930s
B. 1920s
C. 1910s
D. 1940s

17. **What does Al Joad think about constantly?**
A. Music and cars
B. Cars and girls
C. Cars and politics
D. Music and girls

18. **How is Casy killed?**
A. In the Joads' car, of malnutrition and exhaustion
B. In a fight during a labor strike
C. By drowning in a river
D. In a field, of heat stroke

19. **Which of the following is a theme in the book?**
A. Organized labor
B. Child abuse
C. Drug addiction
D. Magical Realism

20. **Which of the following is NOT a theme of the book?**
A. Industrialization
B. Child abuse
C. The American Dream
D. Corporate greed

21. **When did The Grapes of Wrath win a Pulitzer Prize?**
A. 1929
B. 1910
C. 1949
D. 1940

22. **Who is the first in the Joad caravan to die?**

A. Granpa
B. Tom
C. Casy
D. Granma

23. **What does the Ladies Committee think is being stolen?**

A. Toilet paper
B. Sugar
C. Peaches
D. Water

24. **What happened to Tom Joad when he fought with an officer during the strike?**

A. He broke his leg.
B. He broke his nose.
C. He broke his arm.
D. He was arrested.

25. **What happens to the starving man whom the Joads meet in the final pages of the novel?**

A. The police come to help him.
B. He dies.
C. Rose of Sharon breastfeeds him.
D. He robs the Joads.

Quiz 4 Answer Key

1. **(A)** To prevent hunger
2. **(D)** With anger and hostility
3. **(B)** He abandons Rose of Sharon.
4. **(C)** Wages are driven down
5. **(C)** The people, through the Central Committee
6. **(D)** Police had tried to stage a riot.
7. **(B)** The wanted to confiscate the residents' belongings.
8. **(D)** Knowledge of Marxist writings
9. **(C)** Ma
10. **(A)** Picking peaches
11. **(A)** A strike
12. **(B)** By each box they fill
13. **(C)** They are inflated.
14. **(A)** Casy is killed and Tom attacks an officer.
15. **(D)** He eats too many peaches.
16. **(A)** 1930s
17. **(B)** Cars and girls
18. **(B)** In a fight during a labor strike
19. **(A)** Organized labor
20. **(B)** Child abuse
21. **(D)** 1940
22. **(A)** Granpa
23. **(A)** Toilet paper
24. **(B)** He broke his nose.
25. **(C)** Rose of Sharon breastfeeds him.

The Grapes of Wrath Bibliography

Jeremy Ross, author of ClassicNote. Completed on February 13, 2000, copyright held by GradeSaver.

Updated and revised by Caroline Lauer August 19, 2014. Copyright held by GradeSaver.

Harold Bloom. John Steinbeck. New York: Chelsea House Publishers, 1987.

F.W. Watt. John Steinbeck. New York: Grove Press, 1962.

Tetsumaro Hayashi. Steinbeck's The Grapes of Wrath: Essays in Criticism. Muncie, IN: Steinbeck Research Institute, 1990.

Mark Bracher. Literature and Social Justice: Protest Novels, Cognitive Politics, and Schema Criticism. Austin, TX: University of Texas Press, 2013.

"The Grapes of Wrath (1940)." IMDB. 2014-08-19. <http://www.imdb.com/title/tt0032551/>.

Mark Mardell. "Grapes of Wrath Revisited." BBC Documentary. 2014-08-14. 2014-08-19. <http://www.bbc.co.uk/programmes/p024mymp>.

"National Steinbeck Center." National Steinbeck Center. 2014-08-19. <http://www.steinbeck.org/>.

Dave Itzkoff. "No Wrath, but Some Discontent, When Nobel Prize Was Awarded to Steinbeck." The New York Times. 2013-01-04. 2014-08-19. <http://artsbeat.blogs.nytimes.com/2013/01/04/no-wrath-but-some-discontent-when-nobel-prize-was-awarded-to-steinbeck/>.

"Banned Books Awareness: The Grapes of Wrath." Banned Books Awareness. 2012-08-12. 2014-08-19. <http://bannedbooks.world.edu/2012/08/12/banned-books-awareness-the-grapes-of-wrath/>.

Essay Contrasting the Movie and Novel Form of The Grapes of Wrath

by Christopher M. Earhart

John Steinbeck wrote the The Grapes of Wrath in 1939 to rouse its readers against those who were responsible for keeping the American people in poverty. The Grapes of Wrath tells the story of the Joad family, migrant farmers from Oklahoma traveling to California in search of an illusion of prosperity. The novel's strong stance stirred up much controversy, as it was often called Communist propaganda, and banned from schools due to its vulgar language. However, Steinbeck's novel is considered to be his greatest work. It won the Pulitzer Prize, and later became an Academy Award winning movie in 1940. The novel and the movie are both considered to be wonderful masterpieces, epitomizing the art of filmmaking and novel-writing.

Although both the novel and movie form of Steinbeck's The Grapes of Wrath are considered to be American classics, the novel provides a deeper understanding of the story's time and meaning.

Absent from the film, the novel's interchapters provide a greater understanding of the time in which The Grapes of Wrath takes place. First, in the movie it is unclear why the Joads are forced to abandon their farm. It is described very briefly by Muley Graves, leaving the audience in a state of confusion. However, in the novel, Chapter 5 explains exactly why the farmers are forced to leave. In this interchapter, Steinbeck uses a dialogue between a farmer and a representative from a bank; the farmer is forced to leave because the bank, or the"Monster" as Steinbeck says, needs to make a profit, and if the farmer cannot produce any goods to pay off debts, then the bank forecloses the land. This happened to many farmers in the 1930's due to a drought, demonstrating how the novel gives a better understanding of the time. Second, in the movie, the Joads travel down Route 66 to California. The movie does not discuss in depth the vast significance of this route. On the other hand, Chapter 12 of the novel describes how Route 66 is a river of immigrants. This interchapter explains how the thousands traveling Route 66 are refugees from the troubles in the East, giving a better description of the time period. Finally, the movie never describes in depth the economic situation of California during the 1930's. In the movie, the story ends leaving the viewer with the image of California as a land of prosperity. However, the novel attacks the economic situation of California with rage in Chapter 25. In this interchapter, Steinbeck describes how a surplus can make prices so low that the farmers have no income, or how the supply of farm goods can be so scarce that the goods are priced too high to sale. This situation plagues California, and farmers are thrown in poverty. This chapter shows how California is not a safe haven for farmers, but a harsh, devouring environment. The interchapters in the novel form of

Grapes of Wrath describe in detail the time period of the storyline, while the movie leaves the spectators unaware of the actual situation of the migrant farmers in the 1930's.

In the novel form of Grapes of Wrath, Steinbeck uses different literary elements, which are not present in the movie, to provide a deeper meaning of the story. One major element in the novel that is absent in the movie is Steinbeck's use of color and imagery. In the novel, Steinbeck paints a beautiful picture of the landscape in Grapes of Wrath. "The surface of the earth crusted, a thin hare crust, and as the sky became pale, so the earth became pale, pink in the red country and white in the gray country...the sun was as red as ripe new blood." On the other hand, color is absent in the movie. The film is black and white, completely eliminating the factor of the beautiful setting in the story. The next element Steinbeck uses in the novel is symbolism. Steinbeck fills the novel with incredible symbolism, from Tom crushing the grasshopper, to our determined turtle, and also when Uncle John sends the dead baby down the river. These symbols give a deeper meaning to the novel. Tom crushing the grasshopper symbolizes the banks crushing the farms with the bulldozers; the turtle symbolizes the Joad family, constantly struggling to reach California and never giving up; Uncle John sending the dead baby down the river symbolizes Moses being sent down the river as an infant. All these symbols enrich and empower the novel's meaning. However, symbolism is virtually absent from the film. This lack of symbolism takes away from the depth and strength of the novel. The literary elements used by Steinbeck in the novel makes the story richer and more vivid than the dull, vapid film.

The novel form of Grapes of Wrath provides a more sensational experience than the movie. The novel gives the reader a complete feeling of the time period. It describes in every detail the situation of the Joads, as well as other farming families forced to be refugees from their homeland. On the contrary, the film leaves the reader questioning as to what exactly is happening in America in the 1930's. The novel enthralls the reader with its beautiful descriptions of the setting, and its deep symbolism. On the other hand, the film is barren, dry of symbolism and color. The movie is focused solely on the plot, depriving the audience of Steinbeck's unbelievable writing skills. Despite the fact that both the movie and novel form of Steinbeck's Grapes of Wrath are viewed as American classics, the movie is almost insufferable when compared to the wonderful masterpiece in the novel form of Grapes of Wrath.

Essay Four Pages of Fear, Hostility, and Exploitation

by James Boo

Steinbeck's intercalary chapters in The Grapes of Wrath have nothing to do with the Joads or other characters of the novel, but help describe the story in different terms. They are similar to poems, offering different viewpoints of the migration, and clarifying parts of the story that the reader might not understand. An excellent example of this use can be seen in chapter 21, where an examination of the attitudes of migrant Okies and the residents of California reveals the changing nature of land ownership among the changing population of California and gives greater meaning to the fierce hostility that the Joads meet in California.

The first section of chapter 21 explores the plight of the Okies, who are simple people forced to leave their homes when industrial change complicates their lives. Steinbeck writes, "Their senses were still sharp to the ridiculousness of the industrial life. And then suddenly the machines pushed them out and they swarmed on the highways." This statement relates the beginning of the novel, with particular emphasis on the death of Grampa and Granma. When industrial farming hits the agrarian midwest, the Joads are forced off their land and driven to migration, deserting the house in which they have lived for so long. Before long, Grampa dies of stroke. His life is tied to the land and cannot keep up with such rapid change, and when he dies Granma is sure to follow. The paragraph continues:

> "The movement changed them; the highways, the camps along the road, the fear of hunger and the hunger itself, changed them. The children without dinner changed them, the endless moving changed them. They were migrants."

Steinbeck emphasizes the anguish which characterizes change in the Okies, particularly Jim Casy and Tom Joad, who will eventually form workers' unions to rebel against landowners in California. They suffer the anguish of losing their farms and their homes, of being forced to move endlessly and painfully in search of work on someone else's land. The anguish caused by sudden change in land ownership is a major aspect of the novel.

The next section of chapter 21 offers an explanation of the hostility that the migrants meet upon arrival in California. Steinbeck describes:

> "Men of property were terrified for their property. Men who had never been hungry saw the eyes of the hungry. Men who had never wanted anything very much saw the flare of want in the eyes of the migrants. And the men of the towns and of the soft suburban country gathered to defend

themselves; and they reassured themselves that they were good and the invaders bad, as a man must do before he fights."

The mild people of California find in the Okies what they have yet to experience - fear and desperation. Sensing the extent to which the migrants are willing to work, the locals begin to fear for their own jobs, and most importantly, for their own property. In fearful defense, they attack the Okies as marauders who mean to destroy both populations through their desperation. This fear transforms into hostility, which reveals itself in the story through the deputies and managers who abuse and assault the Joads, as well as other migrant families in the workers' camps. Steinbeck goes on to write:

> ". . .wages went down and prices stayed up. The great owners were glad and they sent out more handbills to bring more people in. And wages went down and prices stayed up. And pretty soon now we'll have serfs again."

While the citizens of California are engulfed in fear , the business owners see opportunities to make profit off of both the migrants and the natives. The next paragraph displays the situation in which large fruit canneries drive the small farms out of business by exploiting the desperate workers. As more and more farmers are forced to sell their land, the highways become more and more crowded with migrants, not only from the midwest, but from California as well. This phenomenon only gives credence to the accusations of the natives, fearing for their jobs and their land.

The final section of the chapter is an ominous paragraph which depicts the greed of the companies as the cause of conflict between the workers in California, and the inevitable cause of the companies' downfall. The paragraph reads:

> "And the companies, the banks worked at their own doom and they did not know it. The fields were fruitful, and starving men moved on the roads. . . The great companies did not know that the line between hunger and anger is a thin line. . . On the highways the people moved like ants and searched for work, for food. And the anger began to ferment."

The consolidation of land under large companies is ultimately the cause of strife among the Okies and the Californians. However, it will ultimately become a cause of strife for the companies. The fermenting anger is evident throughout the novel within conversation among the Okies, especially that which involves Jim Casy and Tom Joad. When Casy dies and Tom leaves the family to carry on his work, Steinbeck foreshadows that Tom will lead his people to unite against oppression, and this action is what most frightens the companies and banks. The 'fermenting anger' which Steinbeck describes also relates to the novel's title, as grapes serve as a symbol of the migrants, and the wrath represents their anguish and hardship. The thin line between hunger and anger is broken by the changes in land ownership, and retaliation of the workers is the inevitable result.

Within four pages, Steinbeck greatly clarifies and expands upon his story by examining the different emotions and reactions of his general character groups. He takes two sides of an argument and applies them to a third body rather than pit them against each other. By mastering the use of the intercalary chapter, he is able enrich his story with deeper thought and explore it outside the boundaries of his main characters. In this manner, Steinbeck is able to write a four-page chapter which holds great meaning to a 581-page novel.

Printed in Dunstable, United Kingdom

63752755R00067